Mushroom Medicine

The Healing Power of Psilocybin & Sacred Entheogen History

Brian Jackson

Published by FastPencil

Published by FastPencil
307 Orchard City Drive
Suite 210
Campbell CA 95008 USA
info@fastpencil.com
(408) 540-7571
(408) 540-7572 (Fax)
http://www.fastpencil.com

The author is in no way encouraging anyone to illegally harvest or consume psychedelic plants or fungi. He does, however, realize they've been consumed for thousands of years before him, and will be for thousands of years after he's gone. Thus, it's important for those who may find themselves in the presence of a psychedelic, to have the most possible information on the subject available to them with the goal of reducing harm and increasing safety.

Printed in the United States of America.

First Edition

~ To those who dream the impossible dream. ~

❧

CONTENTS

Acknowledgments

Special thanks to my parents, sister Elyse, and close friends: Derek, Patrick, Greg, John, Chris, Stephen, Cory, and Jordan. You've each played a large role in this process. I appreciate your support and friendship more than you'll ever know. It would have been impossible for this story to have taken place without our many conversations and your everlasting encouragement. Thank you.

Cover Art: "Cognitive Universe" by Hameed
http://hameed.deviantart.com
Hameed@gmail.com

Ginger Software: http://www.gingersoftware.com

PREFACE

I've known many people over the years who've taken magic mushrooms recreationally, but very few have taken a large dose in silent darkness as the famed psychedelic explorer Terence McKenna spoke of. Though it had been nearly ten years since I'd taken mushrooms personally, I spent close to 12 months researching the Amazonian brew, "ayahuasca" prior to taking psilocybin again. Due to a busy work schedule which didn't allow for a quick trip to Peru, I was lucky enough to come across a considerable amount of psilocybin mushrooms near my home. After taking a large dose of psilocybin, my entire outlook on life changed dramatically for the better.

While most of my friends could notice an improvement in my personality immediately after the large dose, I still felt there was much more to say. I initially began writing this book strictly about my personal encounters with psilocybin, but quickly realized that I made more sense to doubters when my story was compared with known medical and historical information on magic mushrooms. During the year I collected over 40 used books on entheogens, mushrooms, ayahuasca, and various psychedelics. I also spent countless hours watching lectures, documentaries, podcasts, T.V. shows, and even more time reading articles, blogs, forums, and other information on the subject.

The majority of the hero dose chapter was written the day after my encounter, while the experience was still fresh in my mind. I continued to write 500-1,000 word entries at the 30, 60, 90, 180, and 365 day marks as a way to better gauge my progress long term. A major reason for writing down my experiences was to describe the differences between high and low doses. Taking a large dose of psilocybin the ancient shamanic way provided a new understanding of the medicine than what I had expected going in. It was completely different from anything I'd been through at low or medium doses in the past.

As I spoke with others, most seemed to think they'd taken a higher dose, but few actually had. I soon realized that very few individuals I knew personally had taken mushrooms in a positive set and setting, plus many hadn't even weighed their doses. It appeared to me as if psilocybin was being used mostly for recreational purposes. While I knew these encounters could be fun and even enlightening, there was a much more beneficial side to psilocybin that I felt was being almost completely ignored.

During this time, I also began to reminisce about taking psilocybin during my college years and began questioning the possible effects they had on me growing up. I compared the various doses I'd taken over the years, to the experiences that followed. Before I knew it, an early version of this book began to take shape. My goal was to present as much information on the subject, in the most accurate way possible.

The ideas and information described in this book could not have been written without years of prior research by many authors, researchers, and psychedelic explorers. Countless hours and energy have been spent by these individuals to help us gain a better understanding into the medical, spiritual, and even recreational use of psilocybin mushrooms. These great explorers have often had their reputations and sometimes sanity questioned by those unwilling to think outside the box. In no particular order, I'd like to say a special thank you to: Maria Sabina, R Gordon Wasson, Timothy Leary, John Marco Allegro, Carl Ruck, Dennis & Terence McKenna, Rick Doblin, Roland Griffiths, Joe Rogan, Amber Lyon, Albert Hofmann, & Graham Hancock.

"There is a mind more perfect and more thoroughly cleansed, which has undergone initiation into the great mysteries, a mind which gains its first knowledge of the first cause not from created things, as one may learn the substance from the shadow, but lifting its eyes above and beyond creation obtains a clear vision of the uncreated One. So as from him to apprehend both himself and his shadow… If, however, thou art worthily initiated, and canst be consecrated to God and in a certain sense become an animate shrine of the Father, instead of having closed eyes, thou wilt see First. Then will appear to thee that manifest One, Who causes incorporeal rays of shine for thee and grants visions of the unambiguous and indescribable things of nature and the abundant sources of other good things" Philo of Alexandria[69]

INTRODUCTION

When most people think of psychedelics, especially magic mushrooms, life changing medicine usually isn't the first thing to come to mind. The term "magic mushroom" was first heard by westerners in 1957 through an article featured in Life Magazine. Soon after, it became one of the most iconic phrases of the 1960's counter-culture movement. Many famous people have taken magic mushrooms including: George Clooney, Bob Dylan, Mick Jagger, Keith Richards, Bill Hicks, William Burroughs, Willie Nelson, all four Beatles, Paris Hilton, Sting, Alan Watts, Ozzy Osbourne, and members of the bands Pink Floyd and Muse, amongst countless others.

The effects of psychedelic mushrooms can be attributed to a unique substance they contain, called psilocybin. Psilocybin is a psychedelic compound in the tryptamine family, which closely resembles serotonin. Psilocybin has been classified as a Schedule 1 drug in the United States and is illegal in many other countries. As with marijuana, there's never been a known overdose from this naturally occurring substance. Psilocybin itself is actually quite safe to consume, but like all psychedelics, the users set and setting play a large role in the outcome of the overall experience. In a comfortable environment, at the proper doses, the encounter can be euphoric and even mystical. If taken in the wrong setting, occasionally psilocybin mushrooms can produce paranoia, anxiety, and fear. As a result of poor understanding of the drug by many early users and the government's fear of their possible misuse in the future, a negative stigma was formed around psychedelic drugs that's been hard to shake for almost 50 years.

"Psychedelics are illegal not because a loving government is concerned that you may jump out of a third story window. Psychedelics are illegal because they dissolve opinion structures and culturally laid down models of behavior and information processing. They open you up to the possibility that everything you know is wrong." - Terence McKenna[68]

The only thing I've ever wanted in life was to be part of something that could help save humanity from the wrongs of the world. Whether that was ending wars, poverty, hate, depression, misery, injustice, or any events that take away from our progress as a species, I've always felt that one day I'd be able to use my mind to play a role in helping to defeat these negative forces. I often stay awake all night thinking about ways to solve the world's most unsolvable problems. I've spent more time than most trying to figure these things out, I have no doubt. During this constant quest for knowledge, I've stuck my neck into the darkest aspects of humanity often and on purpose. While I've rarely been afraid of anything that I could physically see in front of me, various events slowly destroyed my confidence and faith in the everyday world. These negative memories seemed to stick with me far more than the good ones. Eventually, I just wanted to be left alone. It soon became easy to rationalize my actions as a way of protecting myself from the next possible soul crushing moment, always lurking just around the corner.

I had a ton of fun growing up and couldn't have imagined feeling as bad as I did by 30 when I was a kid. No single event can be traced to the start of the change, but I had many small negative moments that I could never rationalize enough to fully get over. If I had a bad night at a certain restaurant, I'd never go back. If I learned my ex took her date somewhere in town, it became a place I'd never go again because I could not kick my initial thoughts enough to have a good time. For years, there were only few spots I avoided, but eventually there were only a few places remaining where I felt comfortable at. It was a gradual process, slowing becoming more prominent over the course of ten years.

For much of that time, it seemed no matter what I did or how hard I tried, something would crash down on me and ruin my progress. Even though I was a nice person in everyday life, for the most part I had myself in mind deep down. My ego and importance as a person was still the motivating factor in my decision making then. I would get jealous of others successes and compare my situation to theirs, as a gauge of my progress. Each year was one step forward, two steps back, until I was so far from where I wanted to be, that I quit participating in life almost altogether. I'd always assumed some type of accomplishment, lucky break, or good news would snap me out of it, but it never seemed to happen.

At its peak, I went to work, came home, rode my bike and didn't do much more outside of the house over a two year period. The bike was the only place where I was able to get some sort of peace of mind. If one rides, fast enough, long enough, you will humble yourself physically if nothing else. When your legs are on fire, it's easy to temporarily forget about the stresses of life for a while, so I rode often.

I had NFL season tickets for two seasons, but never attended a game. Something simple to most, like going to out to eat at a local restaurant, became all but impossible for me at times. I lost many friends and missed out on numerous opportunities because of this built up depression and anxiety. After years of thinking that nothing could possibly help, I took what's considered a large dose of psilocybin mushrooms and more than years of personal struggle was solved in a single 4 hour session. The goal of this book is to share my story in support for the use of psilocybin as a medicine. We will also explore the most current medical research to date being done with psilocybin and look into its possible role in the formation of early religion. There's something truly magical about psilocybin mushrooms that we still haven't quite figured out. Those unknown mysteries have always drawn me to them.

"It's a very salutary thing to realize that the rather dull universe in which most of us spend most of our time is not the only universe there is. I think it's healthy that people should have this experience."
- Aldous Huxley[67]

1

My Past Psilocybin Experiences

I grew up in a suburban community located in Central Florida. My family had property that was located near 80 acres of prime Florida cow pasture. It was divided in half by a creek, leaving approximately 40 acres of land on each side. We had an agreement with the original owners, which allowed us to explore his land, as long as we didn't harm the cows or leave garbage on his property. As a kid, my dad and I would spend hours in the field catching and identifying bugs, snakes, butterflies, turtles, frogs, and any other critter we'd come across. I learned what each animal ate, how they lived, how they moved, and what their enemies were. We'd take homemade fishing poles back to the creek and catch largemouth bass, bluegill, bream, and catfish. When the water level was high enough, we'd do cannon balls off the edge into the deeper spots. There was wildlife everywhere back then. One spring, I caught over 30 baby banded water snakes in a single afternoon (and a few water moccasins as well). Near the creek sat a small pond, which was covered in green plant life. There we'd catch enormous softshell, snapping, musk, and painted turtles, much bigger than I've seen to this day.

As a teenager, the pasture became not only my nature getaway, but also a driving range while I was trying my hand at golf. One afternoon, I jumped the fence with a few clubs and a bucket of golf balls. The cows were a safe distance away, and in the opposite direction from where I was aiming. For some reason, on that particular day, the cows thought my bucket of golf balls were buckets of their food. They began to moo back and forth and within a few seconds, 100 or more cows were sprinting full speed at me. I started to run towards the house, but didn't have time to make it back over the fence. As they neared, I turned around. A single young bull with its horns trimmed, charged and knocked me to the ground. From my back, I swung the golf club and yelled, scaring the remaining cows back, without harming them. Luckily I was able to get away and made it home. My forearm was gouged fairly well and I still have a nice scar from the incident more than 15 years later. I'm still not sure what happened that day to cause them to charge. I went back there numerous times with buckets and while they were always curious, no other cow ever acted so aggressively. Most of the time, they could even be hand fed from our back fence.

I'd camped at the creek with friends, and even stayed the night alone well before I was 12 years old. For 10 years or more growing up, I visited this particular pasture many times each week. As I got older, my friends and I would go fishing, drink beer, and camp for entire weekends out there. Many times using this as a spot to take our dates. It was a great secluded place where you could have a campfire and play music with no real chance of getting in any trouble. Almost everyone who visited the creek thought it was one of the coolest places they'd ever been. At school, I would make sure my friends knew to clean up after themselves if they went alone, but always advised others against going without someone who knew the owner.

Though I'm sure I walked past thousands of psilocybin mushrooms on this land over the years, I never once went out looking for them. None of my close friends were into them at the time and I wasn't sure what to look for specifically. I liked having a good time by drinking and smoking pot, but the idea of possibly eating a poisonous mushroom scared away any thoughts I had of trying to find the correct ones. When I was 19 years old, one of my closest and most reliable friends called from college in Orlando - telling me that he'd taken magic mushrooms with a friend and thought I should try them. He knew I loved 60s and 70s music, particularly The Beatles and Pink Floyd. He thought I would be the perfect candidate for them, and enticed me by saying they would give me an entire new appreciation for music and nature.

Now curious, I had numerous questions. Over the next few weeks, he sent me information and I researched quite a bit myself. I don't believe any other human on the planet could have convinced me to take mushrooms at that time besides this particular friend. He was a highly intelligent guy, usually on the safe side, and was extremely confident in a positive experience taking place. We'd been close for years and I trusted him, so we decided to take some together as soon as possible. The only problem was, where would we find the mushrooms? He'd taken them with a different friend, but that option wouldn't be available to us anytime soon. During our conversations, we thought that they may grow in the field near where we'd camped out behind my house, but were unsure. In already knowing what to look for, he came to town and went out hunting one afternoon while I was at work. By walking the tree line for an hour or so, he found just over 20 caps, of various sizes. When he showed up at my apartment with a bag a shrooms, I was amazed by how simple the process had turned out to be.

It was game on. Back at my apartment, we decided to consume the psilocybin by making mushroom tea. Part of our reason for choosing to make tea was to compensate for some caps being more or less potent than the others based on size. By mixing them together, we'd get more of a truly even dosage. The second reason was that I honestly didn't think I'd be able to get them down, due my horrible gag reflex. The idea of eating a fresh mushroom that was growing from a cow pie hours earlier wasn't very appealing to me. We called a trustworthy female friend to watch over us, just in case anything negative happened. Though I didn't understand the value of set and setting at the time, it was the perfect situation and she was the perfect type of person to act as our guide.

We boiled water, put tea bags in a pot, and added the shrooms. To help with the taste, we added sugar and made sweet tea. We then strained the mushroom pieces out and divided the liquid and remaining boiled caps between us. The strained mushrooms were taken like a pill and chased with a drink of tea. My gag reflex kicked him, but I managed to keep it down. Initially, I wasn't sure if I could take a second sip. I thought, *"You're halfway there, just get it over with as quick as possible."* I composed myself and drank the remaining tea in a few large gulps. It didn't taste great at all, but wasn't nearly as bad as I'd expected either.

I was advised by my friend that we'd begin to notice the first effects in 45-60 minutes. Approximately 40 minutes after consuming the tea, right on queue, I started feeling the first effects and laid down on the couch. The texture of my popcorn ceiling began to twist and turn into various shapes ever so slightly. Looking up, I saw a face that would change when I blinked. After opening and closing my eyes, it seemed as though the roof was only a foot from my face. Laying there, the face went from happy to startling in a flash. The change actually caused me to jump slightly. Looking again at the scary face, I immediately found it funny because I knew that whatever happened was only because I was on psychedelic mushrooms. I was aware enough to know my ceiling wasn't really made of faces and the room was clearly more than two feet tall. My friend told me we should walk around outside before it fully hit to look at various plants and animals in nature. I remember physcially having trouble getting down the stairs, but still laughing about the situation given the state of physics at the present moment. Though we'd planned to go further, we didn't make it far, choosing to sit on the corner of the steps, under an enormous old tree. Looking up,

I saw the branches move in a way I'd never seen before. I noticed movement in every branch, limb, and leaf individually, yet still as a single entity. A bird moved from branch to branch as this was taking place, seemingly in its own world, oblivious from the tree's movement. We also looked at numerous insects and gazed into the newly dark sky. I saw an ant carrying a leaf more than triple its body size, which temporarily gained my full attention. Even with light pollution from the city, the stars that night were as bright as any time I can remember.

After nearly an hour of observations, we went back inside, cut the lights, and each laid down on separate couches, while our female guide sat in a chair. We were nearly 1.5 hours into the trip and just hitting the best part. My first encounter with mushrooms was what I'd now call a solid medium dose. In dried weight, we'd taken maybe 3 or 4 grams. We began to listen to Pink Floyd's classic album, *Dark Side of the Moon.* The record starts with a faint heartbeat, which slowly gets louder during the first minute. I now felt as if the room had a pulse, even after the heartbeat in the song faded into the music. While the music played, each song presented a different visual. During an individual song, each note could change the colors and shapes dancing in my mind. Certain sounds were blue, others yellow, and then a red landscape appeared, followed by a green swirl. I was able to hear aspects and sounds in the songs that I'd never heard before, even after hearing these same songs many times prior.

At some point unknown to me, the first CD ended, and our guide put on the next album on our list, which was *Magical Mys-*

tery Tour by The Beatles. For a period of time between the ending and beginning of albums, 10-20 minutes at most, I don't remember much of anything, but did notice the albums were different a few songs into the second record. Similarly to the previous album, the same songs I'd heard all my life, now popped with amazing new sounds and faint background harmonies that I'd never recognized before. *Magical Mystery Tour* ends with the phrase "*Love is all you need*" repeating as the song fades out. We'd only provided our guide with two albums, so upon the second ending, our guide turned on the light and my friend and I both sat up. The effects had worn off a few minutes earlier for him and he'd been quietly waiting in the dark for the same to occur to me. It seemed as though I instantly snapped back into reality. I remember giving him a hug and saying, "*Wow! Thanks man! That was amazing!*"

We then discussed our thoughts on the night. What we saw, how we felt, and how music and psychedelics went together. We also talked about how few people have had that same experience compared to the average population. At the time, one of the most noticeable aspects of the night was in snapping back to reality so quickly. When you get drunk, it takes time to sober up. If you get high, the feeling goes away in a few hours, but still may linger for a while. It took me a few minutes to get my legs and body to feel normal, but very soon after, maybe 15 minutes at most, I felt as though I was completely back and sober. It amazed me that I could be seeing colors and essentially in another world one minute, and a few minutes later, be back in my apartment as if nothing had happened. I felt completely drained though, almost like the end of a long day of work. We felt so incredibly sober, that an hour later, we drove across town to a completely random pasture and went out looking for more. The open parts of the field were flooded from a recent rain and there were wild boar moving among the shadows in palmetto bushes. After a few minutes, we quickly learned that this wasn't the place or time to be out picking. We decided to head back and called it a night.

The ease in which my friend found so many of those first mushrooms, very close to my home, made me think we'd probably be able to find more whenever we liked. A few weeks later, the two of us went out to the pasture again, only finding three mushrooms in total. We decided not to pick them in hopes of finding more another time in the near future. We'd both been rambling on to our friends about our magic mushroom trip in the weeks since first taking them. From sharing our story, we found ten or so like-minded people who wanted to try them as well. Over the next few months, we kept looking for more, both together and individually. We also asked others for any tips that may help us in our quest. Unfortunately, very few people in our group of friends had the slightest clue of what to look for or where.

One time after hearing a solid tip, we went to a town many miles away to hunt with a group of five students, in a very promising location. This was a well-known mushroom spot, commonly foraged by many in the Orlando area college crowd. We were told exactly where to go on the property, but after having car issues and spending 2 hours in the field, we came away empty handed. Three of the group, myself not included, went back out the following day. Upon finding enough mushrooms to fill a plastic grocery bag, they were forced to drop the shrooms after a neighbor called the police on them for trespassing. It was a close call. Given the location and the severity of the officer's threats, they didn't even take the chance to go back and retrieve their stash. I continued to visit the pasture near my parents three or four times each summer over the next few years. Many times, there weren't any mushrooms growing at all and at best, maybe only a few. I searched the entire field each time, but they seemed to only grow in one specific area for the most part. On close to 80 acres of land, the mushrooms were only prominent in a section of about two acres with any regularity. Looking back now, I realize that in many instances we'd searched in the incorrect spots or even during the wrong seasons. I really didn't put too much thought into it as it was never my primary reason for going to the creek. I enjoyed seeing the animals and liked to compare how the land looked then, to how I remembered it growing up. The mushrooms, if they happened to be there, were only a lucky by product of going out to one of my favorite spots in nature.

Even with that mindset, I got lucky a few times on my own. One afternoon I found seven caps, with four of them being rather large. After not finding enough mushrooms for a decent trip many times prior, I decided to do these alone. With my friend, we'd split 20 or so caps. I assumed for one person, 10 medium caps would put me close to the magic number. I didn't even think to weigh them back then because I was strictly focused on finding a similar amount to the first time.

I told a few close friends that I'd be taking mushrooms alone, which made them immediately assume something bad would happen. The unanimous thought was someone else should be there with me, just in case. Against their advice, I made the leap by myself. It felt better that way, as I wasn't keen on another person watching me without also taking some. I had such a great first time, that I had no fear of having a bad trip in any way. I felt that whatever happened, it wasn't "real." By forming this attitude early and having a strong curiosity to explore my mind, there was seemingly nothing to be afraid of.

So again, I made tea and managed to get it down. I then turned off my living room and kitchen lights, while leaving a dim hallway light on a few rooms away. After some time, I began to notice slight effects beginning to take place. I put on a Jimi Hendrix song and grabbed my guitar. It probably would've sounded terrible had anyone else been in the room, but to me, it felt as though I was nailing every note right along with the music. The vibrations from the strings could be felt throughout my body and more in my fingers than any time I'd played in the past. I stopped the music and begin to play single notes on the fret board. I'd dabbled with a guitar for years, but never understood music theory or chord progressions. I'd memorized and could repeat a few chords, but didn't understand octaves or scales. Though I didn't become Clapton overnight by any means, something in the way the music felt in my hands, made me a much better guitar player forever, from that moment forward. The best way I can describe it is that I could feel little connections between various notes on the fret board, and some combinations just made more sense in some way than others. After a few minutes of practice, I was able to find many patterns hidden in the strings that I'd never picked up on before.

There was a famous Pink Floyd poster on my wall, which had six of their album covers painted on the backs of naked women. While looking at the poster from 15 feet away, the girls seemed to come to life, whispering to each other, giggling, but never completely turning around to look at me. I was fascinated by how they'd become animated. I noticed that various other pictures or posters did the same, moving in unique ways amongst the dimly lit room. I also saw similar movement within the popcorn ceiling as I had during my first experience. The normal formation of my ceiling began to swirl, move, and interact with each other so that it appeared in many ways, to be alive. It's not the same spinning one commonly relates to having too much alcohol. On psilocybin, it's more shapes and shadows moving around, bouncing off one another slowly and peacefully, causing the user to want to see more. After too much alcohol, one usually chooses to close their eyes in order to keep the entire room from spinning to a point they get sick.

For the rest of the night, I had more of a nature themed trip, both in and outdoors. Wind, water, and again, numerous plants and countless trees became the focal points. Seeing wind form waves on a lake blew my mind temporarily. A particular toad jumped, almost in slow motion, much further than it originally appeared to be able. During a point in the evening, I watched my cat move around the house and felt he was much smarter than I'd previously thought. That same night, I studied my fish tank for an hour, face to the glass, in awe of how the various animals inside could move through a liquid in the ways they do. Though, I'd grown up loving nature, psilocybin gave me an entirely new appreciation of the natural world. After about 3 hours I realized the effects were slowing down and by the 4th hour, it was as if I'd never taken anything. Overall, the experience was great, but I'd definitely taken a slightly lower amount than my first time trying psilocybin mushrooms. It was the same movements, shadows, and feelings, but somewhat more thought provoking, with slightly less visuals than before. I had more control to think about what was taking place at a given moment during the night. Whereas the first trip, I was on my on a couch, watching a show, with almost no control over what I'd see for the most part.

I've felt nauseous on mushrooms and had some startling moments, but have never had what I'd consider to be a bad trip. Most uneasy sick feelings are in the first 20-40 minutes as the process begins. One may also sweat and your nose will run during this time. To a certain point, your mind tries and is able to resist the change. As Terence McKenna advises, it's best to take a high enough of a dose so that you aren't able to resist. The quicker this occurs, the easier the process becomes. I've only thrown up once while taking mushrooms, and that was because the environment was completely incorrect. That time we'd split 12 nice sized caps amongst 3 people. The problem was it was a party atmosphere. There were lights on, too many people moving around and I'd had a few beers hours earlier. We put on The Beatles movie, *Yellow Submarine* and within 30 minutes, the psychedelic colors on the TV made me sick to my stomach. Even after getting sick early on, I felt great for the rest of the evening. I didn't see much that time, but could still feel a slight difference in the room over the course of the next few hours. For the most part, the group of us just laughed about any and everything that night.

Though I'd always taken mushrooms recreationally, they were never something I felt I needed, or even wanted to do often. They were mostly taken around a specific group of friends, the few times we were able to come across a sizable amount. Over a 3 year period, I had countless similar experiences to the reports in this chapter with psilocybin, averaging at least two or three per year. Of those, the first was always the best time. It was also the largest amount of mushrooms I'd taken in one sitting. Only certain times were done in correct set and setting with what I'd consider a strong dose, which makes those particular instances stand out. To put it best, psilocybin mushrooms were rare to come across and most of the time, we just didn't have enough to go around.

When I was 22 years old, the friend who'd introduced me to mushrooms graduated college and moved 2,000 miles away in search of a career. Though we kept in touch often, I lost contact with many of the people we'd known locally at the time who were into taking mushrooms. Around that age, many of my other longtime friends also began to move away, get married and have children. In growing up and having more responsibilities, we saw each other much less. From then on, when we got together, it was spent having dinner, reminiscing about old times, or grabbing a few drinks. Our weekends were no longer spent tripping on magic mushrooms. For many years prior, members of these groups would come home from local colleges every few months during the summer, Christmas break, or Spring Break. In the past, I would always look for mushrooms in the weeks leading up to seeing them, but once these friends moved, I rarely went out hunting anymore. By then, I felt as though I'd taken psilocybin plenty of times and naively thought that I'd seen just about everything that mushrooms could possibly offer. I continued to speak highly of the experiences for years after and never ruled out taking them again, but without a steady source myself, or others asking me to go look for them, I soon became more interested in other activities as well.

It would be nearly 9 years until I took psilocybin again.

2

Darkness Closes In

Growing up and throughout my teenage years, I was a happy kid with many friends. In school, I kept an A to B average with little effort and excelled at just about every sport I became involved in. I enjoyed reading, nature, and wanted to learn as much as I could about anything I came across. Though I've always been quiet and reserved, back then I was confident and saw the potential in everything I was exposed to. If I was given constructive criticism by a friend or coach, it didn't get me down for long and I would use it as motivation to become better. I've never had many enemies and overall, my childhood was great by most definitions.

There wasn't a single event that changed me, but more of a gradual beat down by everyday life over a 10 year period, with particular moments stinging more than others. The negative events I went through were very common situations that almost every person will face, numerous times, over the course of their lives. For some reason, I was unable to process and move on from certain events. With bigger issues, sometimes I couldn't get to the source of the problem to understand how and why they occurred. I'd replay the events over and over, sometimes for years whenever something would remind me of them.

The first time I remember myself avoiding public situations was around 2004. A girl who I'd dated for a long time became pregnant fairly quickly after our breakup, by a guy who didn't treat her well at all. She came to me for help a few times, and of course this backfired nearly every time. Living in a smaller town, it seemed everywhere I went for months after, problems would arise. Three days in a single week, we had groups of people related to him show up causing problems, looking for fights at various establishments. I was in great shape and worked out every day, but wanted no part in it. I began to go out less, basically just to avoid any possible trouble. It became hard to let go of the resentment I had for these people and places. When I did go out, I was on edge, almost expecting an unseen sucker punch to be thrown at any moment.

A group of mutual friends dissolved around this time and I found myself hanging out with guys from the apartment complex where I lived. Many of them were criminals, who did harder drugs and would steal right out from under your nose. They were much different than my old group of friends. As naive as it may seem, I was blown away that people actually lived and did some the things they spoke of. Those 9 months were essentially a downward spiral of heavy drinking, amongst trying all sorts of new substances that I'd never imagined being around to begin with. After a while, I realized I had to get away from this group. Upon numerous excuses and reasons I couldn't or didn't want to hang out with them, they finally trashed my screen porch while I wasn't home one night.

In the summer of 2004, Florida was hit by three hurricanes in a month and a half. The screen porches on most of the apartments where I lived had been torn up and would remain damaged for months after. Finally, the apartment staff replaced each resident's screen porch and were quite proud of how it turned out. On the night they were fixed, mine was vandalized by the guys I was trying to slowly ease away from. My landlord wasn't happy at all. Though I'd lived there for almost 4 years and was in good standing with the staff, because of that incident, I was asked to be out by the end of the month. I literally moved 3 miles down the road, in the middle of the night, so the others wouldn't know where I lived in the future. Now with even fewer social activities, I spent much of the next year trying to figure out where I was headed.

A new roommate and I came up with our own version of something I'd seen at UCF called a biodiesel processor. For 2 years, we built machines that helped customers turn vegetable oil into biodiesel, safely and easily at home. We put quite a bit of our time and money into the project. Things went great and we had big dreams after the first few sets of processors went out. When diesel was over $4 per gallon, our machines could help others produce biodiesel for $2 or less per gallon. When gas prices suddenly got lower, our customers were less inclined to buy a $1,000 machine to only save a small amount of money on their fuel. The cost to make the processors increased as well, but worst of all PayPal froze $18,000 of our eBay payments due to suspicious activity. I'd sold the items via eBay, on a 5+ year old account with over 300 positive feedback and zero negative marks against it.

In talking with PayPal, they said it was a precautionary measure against fraud that could be resolved quickly by verifying customers were receiving their products. I distinctively said in separate auctions that half would available to be shipped, while the rest were listed as "local pick up only." Brilliantly, PayPal asked for shipping on 3 orders that were picked up locally, which sounds like something that could be fixed easily. Instead, it took faxing them over 45 pages of documentation, bank account records, shipping receipts, and handwritten letters from customers, which in the end, had to be sent to 4 separate times. After hours of phone calls, countless angry customers, and complete ignorance on the part of PayPal, I decided to refund every customer, create my own website and go from there. We managed to get back most of our money, but I was very bitter over this for a long time. It felt like we were so close, even if just for the short term, and it was taken away by others irreversible errors. I felt we had a great idea and amazing product, yet the powers that be froze our money, essentially because we'd done too well too quickly, causing suspicion.

After creating the initial biodiesel website, I began writing blogs on various topics. Though I still worked my full time job as an income tax preparer, after a few years, I had numerous websites, each earning a small amount of money. In the middle of my best income month in four years, without notice, my primary website income was cut in half and continued to drop for weeks after. I'd been attacked by a rival websites black hat SEO campaign. It was nearly impossible to speak with Google in a quick time frame to resolve these issues. I'd written letters and cleaned up anything I could, but they never reinstated my account. It would be weeks before they got back to me with a vague pre-written email response. Another few years of hard work, countless hours each day, and now my part time income was all but gone again. These instances, affected my attitude greatly. My priorities were also skewed to begin with, most days, for a very long time. I began to expect the worst possible outcome in every situation and I began to feel as though the world was somehow working against me.

By this time, I was in another relationship. The girl I was dating was a teacher, and more of an outgoing person than I was. As I got worse about going out, she became more frustrated with me. I was constantly in a bad mood and upset with many of my own decisions. I had another long term relationship come and go, but this allowed me to reunite with my high school sweetheart, who was also recently single. Being older, we didn't play many of the childish games of our past and our relationship progressed over the next few years. She was better with how I was, as she didn't go out often either. In total, including when we were younger, we dated for close to 7 years. She knew me as well as anyone, but even she could only take so much of my antisocial behavior. When she broke up with me, I was caught completely off guard. We'd just come back from a trip to the mountains and had future plans for the months ahead. We'd recently been discussing marriage and even the possibility of having children together. Of all the unknowns and questions I had about life up until then, I'd never imagined her not being a part of mine. At that time, she was the only piece of the new puzzle I had in place, yet was the most important. In being with her, all the other pieces began to make sense and for once, an image of the future bad had been put in front of me that I could again feel slipping away.

I attempted to keep in touch with her for months, hoping that time would bring us back together, but it never came to fruition. That particular relationship ending and how it did, was my final breaking point. It completely broke me in half to where I barely left my house for the next 12 months. In general everything sucked and I couldn't imagine it getting even remotely better. Eventually, I would try to humble myself by comparing my life and situation to a kid in Africa, or woman in the Middle East, or a prisoner in WW2, or a homeless person, or an uneducated person, or an unhealthy person. We have it pretty good, even on our worst days, to be in this country, with these technologies, at our age, in these times. It helped to think like that.

I unwillingly forced myself to start taking random chances, going out, and doing more nice things for other people. For a short time, I was able to go with this and did get out more, but I was completely faking it while I was there. I was not enjoying the moment or doing things for the right reasons, just going out, almost hoping someone else would make the night worth it for me. I was on edge most of the time and could never fully get comfortable. Knowing I may have this uncomfortable feeling made it easy to back out of plans and just stay home. I'd pump myself up about going out with friends, only to justify in 10 different ways why I shouldn't. Even in recognizing there was a problem, this cycle continued on for months. In many instances, people I enjoyed being around, invited me to places and events that I should have been fine with, but I just couldn't get my head in the right place to go. Sometimes I wouldn't go because I didn't feel happy or energized and didn't want to bring down anyone else who may be there. Other times, I allowed past negative memories to keep me away from places I'm sure I would have had a good time at.

I knew I had to fix this and that nothing bad would come from being in public, but over time, even the simple idea of going out to dinner made me feel awkward. Events never seemed worth the effort. Eventually, I could find a reason why every situation would not be worth the struggle and it seemed to be getting worse as time went on. During the next two years, I read every self-help book I could find. I watched lectures on YouTube, talked to others who took medicine for similar problems, and even tried quite a few of them myself. I spent most of my free time reading, writing, and exercising, almost always late at night, in solitude. I became obsessed with politics, spending hours per day watching Congressional debates and various political talk shows. The world appeared impossibly divided to me. Democrat vs Republican. Black vs. White. Gay vs. Straight, etc. The news seemed constantly filled with negative stories, which would then frustrate me ever more.

In time, even my closest friends would jokingly refer to me as a hermit. I knew they meant well, so it didn't bother me until some of my opinions began to be discredited because of my lack of recent experiences. Within the same week, three of the few people I still regularly communicated with, in separate instances from one another, told me that I didn't understand what I thought to be common aspects of the everyday world due to my lack of being in public. Soon, this became a common theme in my conversations with those in all three groups. A normal back and forth civil debate would be taking place and without fail, someone would counter my point with a quick jab, such as, "*Well, you never leave the house, so how would you know?*" or "*I don't think those stats are relevant to you, because you're not out of your house enough to be part of the demographic.*" Though they may have had a point, I took offense, because even though I didn't have a night life, I still went grocery shopping, worked a job, and participated normal everyday interactions with others. I may have felt uncomfortable in groups, or miserable with my past decisions, but for the little time I was out in public, I felt as though I played it off amazingly well. Outside of my little group of friends, no one had a clue about my problems because I didn't want anyone to know.

Unfortunately, the lowest point of those 2+ years was still to come. For the first time in my life, the Super Bowl and my birthday took place on the same day. Numerous friends encouraged me to throw a party at my house for the double event. I started contacting people a few weeks out because I realized they'd make their own plans as the event got closer. I wrote, texted, or called almost everyone I knew. Initially, I only expected 10-12 individuals to attend, but surprisingly, nearly 30 people said they were planning on coming by for the game. Shocked and doubtful of so many showing interest, I confirmed and reconfirmed who'd be attending. The day before my birthday, I went shopping and bought a few hundred dollars worth of food and alcohol for the party. On game day, as kick off time approached, I began to receive the usual birthday wishes, as well as numerous cancellations for my event. Four would-be attendees had decided to watch the game at home. Two other couples linked up and were already on their way to a party taking place in another town. As the excuses continued to roll in, I began to feel worse and worse. Individuals whom I'd expected to be at my place, called during the game to tell me about the other awesome events I was missing. Others who canceled because they were tired or had to work, began to post photos on Facebook, drinks in hand, having a great time somewhere else. 2-3 of my closest friends didn't show up and never gave a reason. In the end, only 2 of the original 30 or so people that I'd invited showed up.

I don't consume alcohol very often, but I easily put back 12 beers that night out of frustration. After my two friends left, I stupidly went for a drive through the back roads of my empty town, with no real purpose other than getting out of the house to think. After an hour or so, I parked on the side of the road, in a familiar subdivision and just completely lost it. I began crying uncontrollably, in a way I hadn't since I was a small child. If no one wanted to be around me on that day, particularly, in those circumstances, then when would they ever want to be around? I took a deep breath and said to myself, "*That's it. I don't ever want to feel how I do right now again. From this point forward, everything changes."* I promised myself that by my next birthday, if I hadn't snapped out of it, I would move as far away as possible and never speak to anyone outside family, from my hometown again. Deep down I knew that leaving would only mask my unhappiness in a new way, but if nothing else, the idea of a fresh start gave me a temporary sense of hope.

I made it home and began drunkenly boxing up my belongings. By the time I went to sleep that night, I'd packed one of my bedrooms, most of my kitchen, and filled 4 garbage bags with items I'd decided to throw away. For the next month, I didn't do much except eat, work, sleep and continue to pack. I didn't speak to any of the people I'd invited to the party for a long time. I had a huge chip on my shoulder. My mindset was, *"If these people think I'm such a hermit, then I'll be a real hermit and they'll never hear from me again."* I'm fairly certain nobody even noticed I was missing during that time.

I kept telling myself that something good would happen soon. I remember hoping that one day I'd be able to look back on this entire situation and laugh. As months passed, I began to realize that no one was going to come save me from myself. I was the only person who could fix this. I could no longer be reactive and hope for something else to bring me back. This situation had to be tackled head on, by myself. I had no clue where to begin and felt as though I'd already tried the most common remedies many times over. With nine months remaining until my next birthday, I began to seriously plan for the move, assuming it was inevitable.

On what was a very normal evening, I went for my nightly 25 mile bike ride and came home to work on an article I was writing for a blog. I turned on The Joe Rogan Experience podcast as I did many nights. The guest was UFC fighter Dan Hardy, who was speaking about an ayahuasca ceremony, he'd recently participated in. During the episode, Joe spoke of what many believe occurs during a psychedelic experience.

"Psychedelics work by forcing yourself to take a hard look at yourself and address some questions you might have one way or the other, but to do it with this stuff that absorbs one's ego. It removes your ego. It's a rare state where you can get the fuck away from your ego, but it really lets you get away from it to a point where you can see things so much more clearly. And you can realize how much of the ego has been sort of tricking you and deceiving you, and making you believe you're either something that you're not or you've gone further than you really actually have. Your ego allows you to sort of delude yourself to get by this very strenuous existence and when you go into a psychedelic state, it allows you to bypass all that and see it." - Joe Rogan[70]

The idea of being able to take a step back and possibly see my situation my from a different perspective had me immediately interested. Prior to that night, I didn't know much at all about psychedelics as medicine. Almost instantly I started feeling something pull me towards ayahuasca. Over the next few months, I watched hours of video and read four books relating to the sacred vine. I became extremely fascinated by the many positive life changing stories being told, but still had the feeling that nothing would be able to solve my personal issues. How could a plant, possibly help me get over my ex-girlfriend quicker? Or cause me to be less nervous in a random line at the store? How could it really make me see anything differently after the experience was over? Though still a skeptic, I felt as though the jungle was calling me. I knew that I had to get to the Amazon and take part in a ceremony soon. The more I learned, the more I wanted to go, but tax season was just beginning. That meant three to four months of long hours, with few days off and no time to travel. I began to look into ayahuasca retreats in January, with hopes of going to Peru sometime during the summer months.

While researching ayahuasca, I came across quite a bit of information regarding other psychedelics as well. Psilocybin mushrooms, Peyote, and LSD were often compared to the ayahuasca experience in various ways. Since mushrooms were the only psychedelic I'd taken before, and thought I knew something about, my spare time after work also became spent reuniting with old Terence McKenna lectures on YouTube. I had a close friend that was an avid fan of Terence years ago, who would randomly quote him on a weekly or even sometimes daily basis. He owned a couple burnt CD's with recorded lectures from what I believe to have been part of McKenna's book, *True Hallucinations.* Back when I first tried mushrooms, we'd listen to these amazing theories and reflections from Terence's trips into the psychedelic unknown, over and over again.

As recently as ten years ago, our only access to McKenna outside his books were a few hours of tapes or internet clips we were lucky enough to come across online. It seems almost everything he's ever said has now been put on the net for us to enjoy. Through these newly found lectures, I came across a repetitive talking point in McKenna's words regarding psilocybin. "*Take 5 grams in silent darkness.*" As mentioned in Chapter 2 of *Food of the Gods,* he explains that different effects are seen when taking a low, medium, or high dose of psilocybin. Essentially a low dose means better vision and a medium dose is more in line with the common mushroom experience, had by many. What interested me most was how he spoke of the higher amounts, sometimes called "hero" or "heroic" doses.

"This third level, then is the level of full-blown shamanic ecstasy. The psilocybin intoxication is a rapture whose breadth and depth is the despair of prose. It is wholly Other and no less mysterious to us than is was to our mushroom munching ancestors." - Terence McKenna[30]

We'd never weighed or dried our mushrooms in the past, so I had no clue what 5 grams dried looked like at the time. The commonly used dry to wet formula can be found by multiplying the dry amount by 10. With this simple calculation, 5 grams dried would equal about 50 grams of fresh picked mushrooms. The reason for this is due to mushrooms being composed of approximately 90% water. I soon began to recall the dosages from my prior experiences. The first time was the most we'd ever taken, and by far the best. If I could at least recreate a time like that it seemed worth trying again. I decided that once the spring came, I would take a walk out to the pasture and see if I could find anything. If I couldn't find enough to do a true heroic dose, I'd pass until the option became available.

3

My Heroic Dose: Into the Abyss

I decided to go picking in late spring, a few days after a heavy rain. My expectations were low given the amount of failed trips and the hit or miss tendency of my previous hunts in years past. Upon entering the field, within the first hundred yards of the entrance, stood one of the largest *Psilocybe cubensis* mushrooms I'd ever seen. Surprised and encouraged, I continued to walk my usual diagonal path toward the creek. After many treks and never seeing a single shroom in this particular area, I was able to find more than enough for one person, just along the initial path. While definitely the correct species, these particular mushrooms were exceptionally bright in color compared to what I'd remembered. The caps were slimy, shining almost, which made them easy to find as they stood out against the dark spots of manure that littered the field. With what I learned later to be 180 grams and content with my findings, I was back in the car within 20 minutes. It was a very simple process and almost felt like destiny.

Arriving home, I decided initially against taking them that night, as I had to work the next morning. I temporarily placed the mushrooms on a paper towel in my refrigerator and went about my afternoon. Later that evening, I spoke with a friend who encouraged me to either dry them, or take them soon because it would be a shame if they were to go bad. It was still early and I had nothing planned, so I decided to make the commitment and take them that night after all. Even in having many prior encounters with magic mushrooms, I had no clue of what was to come.

At 9:20 pm, I removed the stems and cut each shroom into quarters. I stacked a few pieces at a time, set them on my tongue, and took them like a pill with water. I continued this ritual every few minutes until the caps were gone. Then I chopped the stems into smaller pieces, finishing off 55 grams of fresh psilocybin mushrooms in just over 20 minutes time. I listened to a few minutes of a lecture by McKenna, then put on some music and waited.

Just before 10:00 pm early effects were beginning to take place. My stomach felt slightly upset, though seemingly from drinking too much water while washing down the shrooms. Approximately 40 minutes after the first caps were eaten, my nose began running like a faucet. I was chatting with a friend online at this time and went into the bathroom to blow my nose. Upon touching a white sink, small black metallic beads would appear for just a second, wherever my hand made contact. They looked and moved similar to Mercury, except they were shiny and black instead of silver. Upon going back into my room, the walls began to breathe. They seemed to be made of jelly material and pulsated slowly, in and out. The shadows in the room began to make odd shapes and even patterns on the walls.

By the time the second song finished, I was becoming more and more preoccupied with my surroundings. It felt as though I could have jumped inside my computer at any moment. The screen became filled with bright colors and appeared to be in high definition. I was still attempting to chat with a friend online, but my spelling was becoming horrible. My hands had trouble putting the thoughts into words and just when I found the right words, my mind became flooded with even more thoughts. After re-reading some of my misspelled, hard to understand paragraphs, I managed to let him know that I'd speak with him later, after the event was over. From my past encounters with mushrooms, this is usually where it stops intensifying and the above mentioned events continue on for a few hours. I was expecting more of what I'd always discovered on mushrooms: interesting shadows, increased perception, and awesome sounding music. Around 11:30 pm, everything completely changed. Not only the trip, but my entire life from that point forward.

I cut the lights, turned off the computer monitor, shut the blinds and got into bed. I felt this was as close to the shamanic way McKenna spoke of as I could make happen at the time. Even in taking these measures, a small beam of light made its way across the ceiling through the blinds. I was laying on my bed watching the popcorn ceiling move within the shadows, for what was probably less than ten minutes, when I realized everything had gone completely black. Pitch black. The tiny amount of light that was visible just moments before was now gone. Every time I'd taken mushrooms in the past, I'd known exactly where I was. I could walk around while seeing interesting visions, but always knew I was still inhabiting earth. This time was much different though. All signs of normal reality went away and I entered some type of amazing new dimension.

I was suspended in the most quiet, darkest place I've ever been. Simply floating, with zero effort. No movement at all. Not how an astronaut moves in space, but almost as if I'd been stuck in time, completely frozen to this particular spot. I remember realizing the lack of physics present and that I didn't have a body, but I could still use my eyes. In my peripheral vision in each direction, I could see a golden yellow bubble of energy, almost as if I had been placed just out in front of it. The entire source of energy was behind me and to each side, which extended as far as I could see. It looked and moved like the wax inside a lava lamp as a whole, but had smaller bubbles of energy within it, pulsating incredibly fast on their own. To my amazement, this powerful golden entity, then began to communicate with me in various ways.

I was immediately hit by an immense, almost overwhelming feeling of love and compassion. The phrase "*Everything will be alright.*" could be felt over and over without being heard. I can't stress enough how something was directly telling me that everything would be ok. No words, no sounds, but I knew. Next, I got this astonishing sense of comfort and security. At this point, I started seeing images of everything imaginable from different points in my life flashing in front of me. This began slowly, with the first few images only being recognizable for a split second. Soon after, the pictures were changing as if one was flipping pages in a book, where you'd never run out of pages. As the loving feeling continued to grow, the changing images soon became a single object that morphed into the most amazing shapes and colors imaginable. As the kaleidoscope of geometric patterns continued, more incredibly powerful emotions began hitting me. It wasn't the same as we feel when caring for a boy or girl, or being in an earth-love relationship. This was an entirely different feeling from anything I've ever felt. I instantly knew how much my friends and family cared about me on a very deep level. I could feel both the joy and pain I'd caused certain individuals close to me, yet from both mine and their perspectives seemingly at the same time. I saw many of the people I cared for the most in my life, at their best and worst moments. I also began to understand their personal fears and pains individually.

Soon after, I remember feeling as though a huge weight had been placed on my still non-existent shoulders. During this brief moment, I saw many of the negative aspects of humanity today: Starving children, homelessness, bombs, war, guns, and various other forms of violence raced across my mind, almost as a lesson to help remind me how good I had it. I remember trying to turn away at first, but without a body, I couldn't. I then said via thought to the energy, *"Show me everything, I can take it."* I could again feel the mushroom continue to share its wisdom, *"This is exactly how it's supposed to be. There is no reason to be scared, ashamed, or embarrassed about anything. There is absolutely no reason for this. You should never be that way again. Everything's going to be alright."*

At this point, I felt the golden energy behind me get closer and felt that it wanted to be me at that moment, more than anything else. It was happy that I'd come to visit and even proud of who I was as a person. It loved me. The energy bubble was stuck in this endless dark eternity, seemingly looking for any possible way to get back and be part of life on earth. The smaller bubbles began moving feverishly, bouncing off the walls with the excitement of one day exploring our planet in the ways available only to a human. I would imagine having all the knowledge in the universe means little if one can't move, express thoughts, or share feelings in the ways, we as human beings are able to. I knew every part of this energy bubble of love was busting at the seams for that very opportunity. It wanted me to know how lucky I was to have that chance. I feel that everything that's living we see on earth is part of the energy that made it back. That's why the world's such a beautiful place.

It was if I was run through a gauntlet of clichés and clarity. Many of the following ideas are not revolutionary, but they are in line with what I was told during my ego death trip to another dimension.

- We are all one. Everything is connected.
- There's a reason, even if it is unknown at the present time.
- Sometimes it won't make sense, but it's supposed to be that way.
- We're all part of this power and the power is in each of us.
- Humans can change the way we are collectively & live in harmony with the planet.
- It's ridiculous to dwell on the past.
- Everything will be alright.

I was the biggest atheist imaginable prior to taking my hero dose of psilocybin, but since, I now feel that when you die, your energy will live on in some way. I certainly don't have all the answers yet, but if you saw how much energy is waiting to take your place, and the fervor in which it moves, one would better realize the importance of the few days we get to spend on this planet, in human bodies. The iconic imagery, beauty, and feelings were something that could only be described as heavenly. If psilocybin had this effect on me, as an atheist in the 21st century, I can only begin to imagine how early man would have thought after having a similar encounter thousands of years ago.

In an instance, I was back in my room and sat up on the bed. The front of my shirt was covered in tears and my eyes were still wet. I don't remember crying during the experience, but it's certainly possible that I may have. My first thought upon returning was that while lying there watching the images change, wide-eyed, I probably hadn't blinked in 3 hours. The more thought I put into it, I now think I may have cried like a baby for hours, but I honestly have no recollection of it.

As I got out of bed, it took a second to feel normal on my feet. It was 1:20 am, exactly 4 hours since taking the shrooms. I felt somewhat off balance and exhausted, but also extremely calm and relaxed. I went into the bathroom and stared at myself in the mirror. I looked as though I'd been run through the cosmic ringer. My eyes were red, somewhat puffy, and still adjusting to the light. Though I would not have won any beauty pageants at that moment, it felt completely different seeing myself again that first time. I remember thinking my body was only a temporary vessel for my spirit. After now seeing my physical image again, I knew it was far less important than what was inside. I looked deep into the mirror, almost attempting see my consciousness. My pupils felt like tiny black holes, specifically created to devour information directly into my mind. I shook my head and thought to myself, "*That was incredible!*"

After a few minutes, I made my way across the house and drank a few glasses of cold water. The water helped me feel more alert, and less uneasy on my feet. I then walked outside and stood in the grass of my front yard. Barefoot and shirtless, I gazed up at the sky. The moon appeared as if it had been hung in space, similar to how I'd felt during the trip. It was larger and brighter than I remembered. Though it wasn't a particularly clear night, I realized that I could see more stars than usual. It was dark, yet I could see amazingly well by the moonlight alone. I felt extremely confident standing there. Not cocky in anyway, but as if that was exactly where I was supposed to be. Before I went inside for the night, a single car slowly came down the road. As the car passed, I remember thinking, *"There goes another human, on their journey, exploring the planet, just like me. Just like all of us."* It made me feel good that I felt connected to them in some unique new way that I'd never known before.

When I laid back down on the bed, the covers felt more comfortable than ever. It instantly reminded me of Terence McKenna's quote:

"Nature loves courage. You make the commitment and nature will respond to that commitment by removing impossible obstacles. Dream the impossible dream and the world will not grind you under, it will lift you up. This is the trick. This is what all these teachers and philosophers who really counted, who really touched the alchemical gold, this is what they understood. This is the shamanic dance in the waterfall. This is how magic is done. By hurling yourself into the abyss and discovering it's a feather bed." [30]

I'd gone into the abyss, and returned with what felt like philosophical gold. It initially seemed as though I'd fall asleep quickly and was hoping to because I had to be up for work in a few hours. Then my mind began to try and make sense of everything that had taken place in the hours prior. As calm as I felt, I didn't get much sleep that night after all. I now realized there was a distinctly different experience between the lower doses I'd taken in the past, and my first true hero dose. McKenna was right. The difference was night and day. I couldn't believe that more people I knew hadn't done this and if they had, why hadn't anyone told me about it? I would reflect on the night for the next 2-3 hours before finally falling asleep well after 5:00 am.

4

OUT OF THE DARKNESS & INTO THE LIGHT

In the end, I only got a few hours of sleep before work. It was a very long day. I managed to write the initial trip report in the afternoon and had a long talk with a friend, before calling it a day early and getting a full night's rest. The trip and lack of sleep had worn me out, as if I'd put 75 miles in on the bike, back to back days, on little food. I was completely drained, both mentally and physically.

After a long night's sleep, I woke up early and refreshed the following morning, feeling absolutely great. I was especially relaxed, more than I'd remembered being in many years. As I got ready for work, I felt as if my life was full of endless possibilities and I was excited for the world to again be a blank canvas in front of me. I felt carefree, yet still focused and goal driven, much more like I did when I was 15 or 21 years old. I knew everything would be fine and that it was silly to worry as much as I had.

My first social interaction was at a gas station down the road from my home, where I've made small talk with many of their long time employees for years. I would always fake a smile, be polite, and ask how they were doing, but it was only because that's the nice thing to do. In all honesty, I wasn't really interested in what they said most of the time and was just going through the motions as many do. An older lady who'd worked there for years was behind the counter on this particular morning. When I spoke to her that day, my words and smile were sincere. I was fully into our short conversation and I genuinely appreciated her as another person in a way I hadn't in the past. The best way I can describe this is that prior to taking mushrooms, I spoke to others in the way I wanted to be perceived based on thousands of small signals I'd learned to decipher over the years. While knowing your surroundings and picking up useful information from it is a good thing, the level to which I did this wasn't. Instead of acting on my own accord, I was constantly analyzing situations over and over, often without even realizing it. This time, though I was on earth communicating with another human in person, it was almost as if my body was still dissolved somewhere else in how I thought. I didn't even consider how she appeared physically, or how she may think of me because I was trying to speak to the same part of her I'd seen in myself, while looking in the mirror two nights prior.

For lunch, I decided to go to a local restaurant that's usually crowded and there's normally a known wait time. Usually my lunches were based on the quickest, cheapest spot, where the fewest people would likely be. Because of this, many restaurants had been off my radar for years. As soon as I decided I wanted this certain food, there was no second guessing or questioning why I shouldn't go. I waited in line, ordered, and ate at a table directly in the middle of the restaurant no less - and it was excellent.

After work, I called a close friend to tell him about my experience. He was living 35 minutes away, and though I'd declined invitations ten times in previous months, I decided to make the drive and hang out at over at his place. This was big, because for years, I rarely went out of the safe zone of my home town. Usually, I only hung out with this person in a one on one setting, but that night there were 5 people at the house. I didn't mind at all and even made two new friends in the process. I wasn't concerned with anything but being there in that moment, with people I enjoyed being around. I ended up going home much later than normal and had a really good time.

My friend reminded me he had a music show that Friday at a local theatre in town. I'd known about his show for over a month and probably wouldn't have gone any time prior, but I knew it was important to him and I said I'd be there. In the past, I didn't make many future commitments because I didn't want to back out later. If I were to make a commitment, no matter how big or small, I'd think about it constantly until the day it arrived. I also wanted to know the most I could about every situation before I would give a definitive "yes." Between Tuesday night and Friday, I didn't worry about it at all and actually became more excited to go as the event grew nearer. Friday came, I went and was glad I had. Before and after the show, I socialized with other guests and musicians, never once having a negative experience. As with the lady at the gas station, my interactions felt much more sincere during the entire first week.

I did a lot of reflecting the first weekend after taking psilocybin again. I remember laughing to myself about how ridiculous I'd acted during at least half of my life. Yet, there were no feelings of regret. I began to notice all these small changes taking place immediately, though I didn't realize how profound they would be until more time had passed. For years, I'd felt as if every set of eyes, in every room, were all focused directly on me. After taking a heroic dose of psilocybin mushrooms in silent darkness, that didn't happen anymore. I was finally free to be myself, without the worry of gaining others approval first. It was too early to know how long this would last, but I felt better than I had in a very long time. This was the missing piece that I'd spent years looking for and I almost knew it would be a long term change, if not permanent.

The following Friday, I called a different person and invited him to go have drinks and play pool. I'd backed out of our plans to do this more than two years prior and he'd reminded me many times since. I don't think he could ever fully understand why I wouldn't or couldn't go in the past, but we ended up going three times in the first month after I took psilocybin. We never had a bad time. Ironically, an old roommate of mine now works at this same establishment. We've met many of his friends and coworkers, effectively turning a place I'd blocked out years ago, into one of the most comfortable settings in my town today.

Soon after, I visited one of my best friends from high school who lives in Brooklyn. Instead of worrying about leaving home and everything involved with that, I was excited, counting down the days until I left. While I was outside in a group conversation at a Brooklyn night spot, I remember thinking that I could have never done this if I hadn't taken mushrooms. Yet, here I was surrounded by writers and Ivy League graduates, making small talk in a crowded New York bar. I was around more people in those few days than I'd been in years back home in Florida. I never felt anxious or nervous once. It was an amazing time and one of the best weekends of my life.

Upon returning from New York, I continued to reconnect with old friends, try new things, and interact with society even more. I was invited to a birthday party, where there were many strangers and a only a few people I'd met before. Usually, I would have found a nice way to do something one on one for this persons birthday that didn't require me being around a crowd. Based on my previous month of positive experiences, I knew that everything would be alright and I went. I actually ended up staying later than my friend, talking into the early morning hours about history, religion, and politics with a group of like-minded individuals.

The resentment towards the relationship with my long-time girlfriend ending how it did, was by far the issue I had the most trouble dealing with prior to taking psilocybin. While I was on my hero dose, I distinctly remember seeing images of my ex-girlfriend smiling, laughing, and being happy as one of the most powerful moments of my night. Any negative feelings towards the relationship were gone by the next morning and somehow, finally, I was no longer lost on the past. A few months later, I was able to meet with the girl I'd been stuck on for so long in person. We had lunch, made small talk about our lives, and have stayed friends since. As crazy as it may sound, today I have nothing but positive memories when I'm reminded of her.

Since taking the heroic dose of psilocybin, I've been happier, more open minded, and less stressed. I've also met more new people, been in more social settings, and have done more good deeds in general. Anything and everything that I'd been stuck on over the years went away and almost instantly life made more sense. I could understand exactly what happened to put me in the situation that I'd gotten into, from a new angle that I hadn't known before.

I now do more for others because I know it will make them feel better, and in turn, it does the same for me. I also put extra thought into how my actions can affect situations and others' moods. When a person in a bad mood walks into a room where everyone is having a good time, the feeling in the room changes. Likewise, if a group is quiet and a loud person comes in, they change the feeling as well. I attempt to bring as much positive energy into others' lives as I can by being kind. One of my goals is to reduce the possible negative moments in life that I can have direct influence over. Bad situations and events will inevitably happen in everyone's life, at some point, but your reaction can affect the situation more than the initial problem if you allow it to. You have power over your actions. A negative moment can ruin your life, or be the foundation of your success. Being nice and smiling allows you the most opportunities to gain positive experiences in life. I've taken the same mindset since the day after my heroic encounter with psilocybin. From that point forward I haven't been depressed or had anxiety at all. There's always this sense of calmness and reassurance that reminds me everything will be alright.

When I took those mushrooms, I was given some untold secret I'd always been looking for. I have no doubt now that the secret to everything is love. There is a difference in just saying it, as we often do, and fully comprehending what that means. I thought I knew and understood this prior, but I didn't. There are many levels to love. The more love you put off to the world in all aspects, the more it will return to you. Essentially, as The Beatles sang, *"The love you take, is equal to the love you make."* I've told people for years I was John Lennon reincarnated completely as a joke, but now I feel like I know much of what he spoke of on an entirely new level. Lennon is rumored to have traveled to Mexico to meet Maria Sabina, the same Mazatec healer who'd introduced R. Gordon Wasson to magic mushrooms years prior. The ideas and emotions the mushroom gave me was almost exactly in line with the mindset of those involved with the psychedelic movement of the 1960's. It appears obvious to me that taking psilocybin, and psychedelics in general, result in a happier, more loving, peaceful human being.

When I tell my story, many seem to get the impression that I've been sitting around my house, tripping my head off every week since. That couldn't be farther from the truth. One may think that after having such a positive exposure, a person would continue to do them regularly, but to me, this is a powerful medicine, not a recreational drug to be played with carelessly. The trip was so incredibly introspective, revealing, and draining, that I need to prepare myself mentally before going back into that realm again. In the twelve months following my experience, to the surprise of many, I've never felt the need to take another dose.

With that said, I've had days where I was stressed or sad, just as I'd expect the average person to go through. Everything is going to be alright doesn't mean stubbing your toe won't hurt anymore, but it reinforces that what takes place today, good or bad, is just a small piece of the larger puzzle. I dated an old friend this summer who, after a couple fun months decided to get back with her ex. Though it felt familiar, and breakups will never be fun, it didn't take long to erase any negative feelings and look at it only as her trying to find happiness. As much as it didn't make sense to me, I knew there was a lesson to be learned and to keep moving forward. As when I was younger, instead of it keeping me down, the instance motivated me quite a bit.

I will definitely take them again, when I'm ready and the time is right. I have no doubt in that. For now, I'm just enjoying being myself again. I missed out on so much, that now the world looks like a huge toy store and I'm five years old, just walking through the door.

McKenna once said, *"The question is, now that you have this knowledge, what are you going to do with it?"*

For the first few months after the trip, my biggest problem was trying to find a hobby and stick with it, because I was enjoying so many new things. For a long time I had an obsessive personality. Once I became interested in a subject, I'd learn as much as possible about it until I found something new. Now, I don't have enough time in the day to try everything I'd like, but that's a problem that I'm alright having. The way I view the world on a day to day basis has changed for the better after taking this ancient mushroom medicine. I'm not sure if anything else could have given me these results so quickly and I couldn't possibly have imagined such a drastic positive change only a short time ago. As you'll read, mushrooms don't only act as a medicine, but also as a spiritual guide. Psilocybin's a key that can open doors to an entirely new world. An infinite amount of knowledge and understanding awaits those willing to travel into those realms.

5

Psilocybin Medical Research

Though LSD was already being studied by psychiatrists in the 1950s with promising results, it would still take a few more years until psilocybin would be given the same type of examination. In August of 1960, a little-known thirty-nine-year-old psychologist from Harvard, Timothy Leary, traveled to Mexico and experienced psilocybin mushrooms for the first time. Leary would later say he *"learned more about ... (his) brain and its possibilities ... [and] more about psychology in the five hours after taking these mushrooms than ... in the preceding 15 years of studying and doing research in psychology."*[1]

Upon returning to Cambridge, Leary would conduct the first modern studies on the effects of psilocybin with his colleagues Richard Alpert, Ralph Metzner, Aldous Huxley, John Spiegel, Frank Barron, and David McClelland, to be forever known as the Harvard Psilocybin Project. The project was best known for two studies, the Concord Prison Experiment and the Marsh Chapel Experiment (also known as the Good Friday Experiment). In prior studies of the drug, Leary's data showed that after taking psilocybin, 90 percent of subjects felt they learned something of value about the world or themselves, while over 60 percent felt their lives had been changed for the better.[2]

The Marsh Chapel Experiment was conducted to see if psilocybin could invoke an authentic religious experience. A controlled group of ten graduate students from the Harvard Divinity School was given psilocybin, while another group of ten students was given the placebo, niacin. After taking the substances, students then attended a Good Friday Sermon while being monitored by guides. Nearly every student who took the psilocybin reported having an intense religious experience. The most famous of the volunteers in the group was author Houston Smith, who said:

The Experiment was powerful for me, and it left a permanent mark on my experiential world view. (I insert the qualifier experiential world view to distinguish between the way I think and believe that the world is, on the one hand, and the way I usually experience it to be.) For as long as I can remember, I have believed in God, and I have frequently experienced his presence in beauty, in nature, and (less frequently) in the clear light of the void that mystics speak of. But until the Good Friday Experiment, I had no direct personal encounter with Him/Her/It of the sort that Bhakti yogis, Pentecostals, and born-again Christians describe.[3]

The Concord Prison Experiment aimed to explore if psilocybin could be used as a treatment for reducing recidivism rates among inmates. Thirty-two prisoners were given both group therapy and psilocybin over the course of two years. Upon gaining parole, they were monitored to see if psilocybin could be used to help keep inmates from returning to jail. Compared to known prison averages, initially, Leary's findings were quite promising. The study found that less than half of the expected number of test subjects returned to jail. Rick Doblin, founder of the Multidisciplinary Association for Psychedelic Studies (MAPS), would complete a follow-up to the Concord Experiment in the '90s, explaining many flaws in the Harvard Project's analysis. Biggest of all, Leary used recidivism rates of his subjects after only an average of ten months, and compared it to thirty months of expected rates provided by the prison. Instead of an impressive 23 percent reduction rate, it was found to be dramatically lower, at 2.3 percent.[4]

As Leary became more of a mainstream counterculture figure, he would be eventually fired by Harvard for leaving particular classes early and not fulfilling some of his required teaching duties. Richard Alpert was also let go for giving an undergraduate student psilocybin. By early 1963, the largest research project on psilocybin was no more. Over the next few years psychedelic research would essentially come to a halt. Leary would continue to advocate psychedelics in the face of authority to the point where it's debatable whether he may have done more harm to psychedelic research than good. Soon after, The Drug Abuse Control Amendments of 1965 would first make hallucinogenic drugs illegal.

On their way home from Mexico, Leary's girlfriend, Rosemary Woodruff, was found with a small amount of marijuana by U.S. Customs. Timothy Leary claimed the substance and was subsequently given a thirty-year prison sentence in accordance to the Marihuana Tax Act of 1937. Leary appealed the sentence on the basis that the Marihuana Tax Act violated the Fifth Amendment. While awaiting appeal, Leary would be arrested again, this time claiming he'd been set up. *Leary v. United States* would confirm the Marihuana Tax Act unconstitutional in 1969, due to tax stamps themselves being self-incriminating. Because of his disrespect for authority and well-known use of psychedelic drugs, President Nixon was said to have once called Leary *"the most dangerous man in America."* Not to be outdone, the very next Congress passed the Comprehensive Drug Abuse Prevention and Control Act of 1970. Part of this law included the modern system still used to classify drugs in the United States today, the Controlled Substance Act. Under this act, drugs are essentially categorized based on their suspected abuse and benefit level.

The term "controlled substance" means a drug or other substance, or immediate precursor, included in schedule I, II, III, IV, or V of part B of this subchapter. The term does not include distilled spirits, wine, malt beverages, or tobacco, as those terms are defined or used in subtitle E of the Internal Revenue Code of 1986.

21 U.S.C. § 802 (6) [5]

By 1970, psilocybin was listed as a Schedule I drug under the Controlled Substance Act. Schedule I classification means the following:

(A) The drug or other substance has a high potential for abuse.

(B) The drug or other substance has no currently accepted medical use in treatment in the United States.

(C) There is a lack of accepted safety for use of the drug or other substance under medical supervision.

The Schedule I label puts those looking to research these substances into a unique Catch-22. They must often jump through numerous regulatory hurdles in an attempt to get the correct approvals just to obtain and study the substances scientifically. Since the drugs have no proven medical benefits and government regulations make them difficult to study, researchers are often denied the chance to find the very medical benefits that would result in the rescheduling of a substance.

In late 2001 Dr. Francisco Moreno of the University of Arizona Medical Center began the first clinical study in over thirty years on the therapeutic use of psilocybin. His three-year study involved giving nine patients with chronic obsessive-compulsive disorder (OCD) various doses of psilocybin ranging from 25 μg/kg to 300 μg/kg. Each patient received up to four doses in total, none sooner than a week apart. During the procedure, the volunteers wore eye shades and listened to calming music in the presence of a trained investigator. One patient reported increased hypertension and some felt stress at times, but no other negative side effects were seen. At the highest doses of 300 µg/kg, subjects we said to have experienced *"profound positive transcendental experiences such as exploration of other planets, visiting past-life reincarnations, and interacting with deities."*[6] All nine individuals showed reduced symptoms during at least one psilocybin session and up to twenty-four hours after treatment. Though the changes weren't long lasting in most individuals, one participant's OCD remission lasted for six months.

Between 2008 and 2011, new studies were published involving psilocybin as a treatment for anxiety and depression in cancer patients. Researchers from New York University (NYU), Johns Hopkins University, and University of California, Los Angeles (UCLA) led the way, each completing similar yet slightly different experiments on the subject. At UCLA, Dr. Charles Grob, supported by the Heffter Research Institute, led a study where twelve terminally ill cancer patients were given a small dose of 0.2 mg/kg of psilocybin each. The volunteers were brought into a comfortable setting with the intent to have a positive therapeutic outcome. The participants showed reduced levels of anxiety at both one and three months after taking the medicine. Volunteers' moods were also reported to have positively increased for two weeks or more after taking psilocybin.

Common themes reported by subjects included examining how their illness had impacted their lives, relationships with family and close friends, and sense of ontological security. In addition, subjects reported powerful empathic cathexis to close friends and family members and examined how they wished to address their limited life expectancy. We saw remarkable and sustained changes in cancer patients' spiritual dispositions. People's entire sense of who they are has been altered in a positive manner.[7] Dr. Charles Grob, UCLA

Dr. Stephen Ross of NYU also conducted studies to document the effects of psilocybin on anxiety, depression, and pain in cancer patients. Although similar to UCLA's project, Ross used a slightly higher dose of psilocybin—at 0.3 mg/kg—and a larger study group. His findings were in line with the traits frequently seen in many other psilocybin studies. As with the previous tests, patients were asked to lie on a couch, with eye shades, and to listen to relaxing music. Many volunteers reported having deeply mystical encounters and out-of-body experiences that were considered to be life changing. After years of crippling anxiety, the test subjects at NYU have seen dramatic improvements in their everyday life. The symptoms of anxiety are closely related to those of PTSD. Psilocybin helps break up common mental patterns and provides the user a new way to view the world.

At the hospital, they gave me Xanax for anxiety. Xanax doesn't get rid of your anxiety. Xanax tells you not to feel it for a while until it stops working and you take the next pill. The beauty of psilocybin is: it's not medication. You're not taking it and it solves your problem. You take it and you solve your problem yourself. [8]

Nick Fernandez, participant at NYU

The emotional, spiritual and existential distress that can often accompany a diagnosis of cancer often goes unidentified and untreated in cancer patients. Patients who have benefited from psilocybin clinical research have reported less anxiety, improved quality of life, enhanced psychological and spiritual well-being, and a greater acceptance of the life-changes brought on by cancer. It is a welcome development that this promising and novel clinical research model utilizing psilocybin has begun to gain clinical and academic attention.[9] Dr. Anthony P. Bossis, New York University

A Johns Hopkins University study revealed that a single dose of psilocybin encouraged a positive personality change in 60 percent of their study group.[10] The subjects wore blindfolds and were provided a comfortable setting. They were also accompanied by trained monitors, who provided reassurance to any volunteers who experienced fear or anxiety. During the trial, Roland Griffiths and his team were able to determine that psilocybin dosages of 20 mg per 70 kg of body weight were the optimal dose for positive experiences. Patients had a much lower chance of encountering anxiety or fear during the event than when compared to at a higher dose of 30 mg per 70 kg. Two months after the study concluded, 70 percent of the subjects said the encounter was one of the top five most meaningful experiences of their lives. After fourteen months, 67 percent still considered the event in their top five. Clark Martin, a retired psychiatrist who participated in the Johns Hopkins study, had this to say about his high dose psilocybin experience:

Everything became tranquil and calm, and I had the sense that I was floating on a giant bubble. I left the session animated and intellectually stimulated. Today I don't have a sense of death like I used to. I see it as part of the flow of nature. There's grieving and sadness, of course, but what's being lost is this false sense of separateness we create. I don't get too worked up about my illness anymore. My relationship with my daughter is better. I'm also more fully present and empathic when I spend time with my elderly father, who has dementia. [11]

If you weighed 70 kg or approximately 155 lb, the amount of psilocybin administered would have been as follows: 14 mg at UCLA, 21 mg at NYU, and varying amounts up to 30 mg at Johns Hopkins, with 20 mg per 70 kg being considered the "sweet spot."

Between 2008 and 2012, researchers at the University of Alabama at Birmingham (UAB) studied data collected from the National Survey on Drug Use and Health, specifically looking for correlations between mental health and psychedelics. In over 190,000 American adults, those who had a lifetime of psychedelic use were found to be 36 percent less likely to have attempted suicide in the last twelve months. Psychedelic users were also 29 percent less likely to have planned a suicide attempt and 14 percent less likely to have suicidal thoughts. [12] While it's not known specifically why users of psychedelic drugs are less likely to be suicidal, we can look to the aforementioned studies and infer that psychedelics tend to make individuals less depressed and overall happier with their life. Happier people are obviously much less likely to have suicidal thoughts than people who aren't. This research opens the door for new possibilities in the world of suicide prevention.

Despite advances in mental health treatments, suicide rates generally have not declined in the past 60 years. Novel and potentially more effective interventions need to be explored. This study sets the stage for future research to test the efficacy of classic psychedelics in addressing suicidality as well as pathologies associated with increased suicide risk. Dr. Peter S. Hendricks, UAB

In the years leading to my recent encounter with psilocybin mushrooms, I came across many positive articles and reports on psychedelics. After my experience, it initially felt as though something had happened to me that no one could have possibly known about before. Since seeing those amazing sights in an egoless realm of wonder, I couldn't imagine someone else had ever visited that same place. I soon learned that what I went through wasn't unique at all, but almost exactly what happens to most people after taking a medium-to-large dose of psilocybin. For my nonscientific dosage, I went by the infamous Terence McKenna model of taking 5 grams of dried mushrooms (50 grams fresh) in silent darkness. This is what he referred to as the ancient shamanic way. I took 5 grams extra or 55 grams in total. That was done to make sure I would get the full effect, assuming at the time, they may have been slightly higher or lower in psilocybin content.

In the *Psilocybe cubensis* species, depending on variables, 0.6 milligrams of psilocybin per gram of wet mushrooms is a reliable average to dose by.[13] In taking 55 grams multiplied by 0.6 mg of psilocybin per gram, my large dose of psilocybin was approximately 33 mg. At the time, I weighed 170 lbs. Though I didn't know it then, for my size and species of mushroom taken, I'm fascinated that McKenna's model placed my dosage almost exactly in line with the highest dose of 30 mg per 155lbs, recently used at Johns Hopkins.

In 2012, at the University of New Mexico, Dr. Michael Bogenschurtz began the first study on the use of psilocybin in the treatment of alcohol dependency. Volunteers who were concerned about their drinking habits agreed to take a 0.3 mg/kg and 0.4 mg/kg dose of psilocybin four weeks apart. Each had been diagnosed as alcohol dependent prior and was attempting to not consume alcohol until after the testing was completed. Of the ten patients who participated, some quit drinking permanently, while many drank considerably less. The most notable charges were seen in the first week after taking psilocybin. All subjects had fewer cravings, drank less overall, and had more sober days in the week following treatment. Most lost some of their gains by week four, but were still better in these areas than before the medicine was taken.[14] These results are extremely similar to those found in the studies done on LSD and alcoholism in the 1950s and '60s.

In September 2014 Dr. Matthew W. Johnson of Johns Hopkins School of Medicine, in collaboration with The Beckley Center and the Heffter Research Institute, published a study linking psilocybin use with helping long-time smokers quit. The subjects selected had smoked on average a pack per day for thirty years. Volunteers were given two doses of psilocybin, in the amounts of 20 mg per 70 kg and 20 mg per 70 kg over a fifteen-week period. Twelve of the fifteen participants, or 80 percent of the subjects, were able to quit for six months after the treatment. These results more than double the success rate of today's leading "quit smoking" pill, Varenicline.[15] Dr. Johnson said *"Quitting smoking isn't a simple biological reaction to psilocybin, as with other medications that directly affect nicotine receptors. When administered after careful preparation and in a therapeutic context, psilocybin can lead to deep reflection about one's life and spark motivation to change."*[16]

Through support from the Beckley Foundation at Imperial College London, research being conducted on the way psilocybin affects brain function has produced amazing new clues into how this medicine works. For the first time, brain maps are showing that overly reinforced behaviors and brain patterns can be broken up and viewed differently under psilocybin. By breaking these habits, new ways of relaying information are allowed to take place. Those diagnosed with depression, anxiety, or PTSD often have traumatic events hardwired into their thought process. After repeating the same processes over and over, it can become difficult for the brain to bypass some of these negative events. When too many connections are formed in the brain, these thoughts can be overwhelming. When an individual takes psilocybin, their brain actually loosens its grip on the usual way the mind pieces together this information. [17] Common brain patterns become followed less and new connections are formed, creating a different way to view the world. Similar research into psilocybin and brain function is taking place between the University of Zurich and The Heffter Research Institute. By learning more about how psilocybin affects brain patterns, researchers hope to follow up on the University of Arizona study on OCD. Overall, these studies being done on psilocybin are providing an enormous amount of new insight into the substance. In every medical study done to date, the results have been positive and appear extremely promising.

Learning about the mechanisms that underlie what happens under the influence of psychedelic drugs can also help to understand their possible uses. We are currently studying the effect of LSD on creative thinking and we will also be looking at the possibility that psilocybin may help alleviate symptoms of depression by allowing patients to change their rigidly pessimistic patterns of thinking. Psychedelics were used for therapeutic purposes in the 1950s and 1960s, but now we are finally beginning to understand their action in the brain and how this can inform how to put them to good use.
[18] Dr. Robin Carhart-Harris, London Imperial College

A nonhuman study on psilocybin was conducted by Dr. Juan Sanchez-Ramos at the University of South Florida. His promising research shows neurogenesis and reduced anxiety towards preconditioned fear in mice that had been given psilocybin. After hearing a specific tone, a group of mice were shocked by a small amount of energy. Soon they would learn to anticipate the shock, freezing whenever they heard the sound, even when the shock didn't take place. The mice that were given psilocybin stopped fearing the shock at a quicker rate than the controlled group.[19] This is the first study to show psilocybin having a similar positive effect psychologically on another mammal. Creating neurogenesis in particular areas of the brain could drastically change the way mental health is currently treated.

Psilocybin enhanced forgetting of the unpleasant memory associated with the tone. The mice more quickly dissociated the shock from the stimulus that triggered the fear response and resumed their normal behavior. The result suggests that psilocybin or similar compounds may be useful in treating post-traumatic stress disorder or related conditions in which environmental cues trigger debilitating behavior like anxiety or addiction.[20]Dr. Juan Sanchez-Ramos, USF

Though Norman Zinberg coined the phrase "set and setting," most first heard the term from Timothy Leary in the '60s. Terence McKenna was one of the first to describe the various effects of high-dose psilocybin in a way it made sense to a large audience. In the last ten years, researchers have discovered that intent plays a role as well. Though I'm positive others have said the same many times, it seems that user intent may be just as important as set, setting, and dosage.

While many individuals may cross over into other statistics, even being counted for two or even three times (for instance, a person with depression and anxiety who smokes), I believe a significant portion of society could benefit from the use of psilocybin in a medical setting. At this time, hundreds of patients have been treated with psilocybin at some of the best universities in the world, with amazing results. Due to the success of these early studies, psilocybin has been getting much more attention in the mainstream media. Just over a two-year period, psychedelic research has been featured numerous times on CNN, The Huffington Post, The New York Times, Business Insider, The Telegraph, The Guardian, The Washington Post,

MSNBC, The New Yorker, and even Fox News. I've felt the life-changing results that psilocybin can offer in regards to anxiety and depression, and I predict that in the coming years, as research continues, it will become even harder to deny the positive effects of this medicine.

The idea of a good doctor is to get rid of you. He doesn't want chronic patients. Poor people, always hanging on to him, always rushing for help. He wants to set you back on your feet. That is an excellent principle. This is where the doctor really has something to say to the priest. Priests tend to, by enlarge, keep you coming back, so you'll pay your dues and the church will prosper. The more people they can get hooked on religion, the merrier. Priests ought to learn from the doctors and try to get rid of them, where they tell their gospels and say, "Now you have it, go away." The faster a doctor can get people out of his office, they'll go around saying, "That man cured me, I didn't have to go back to him." More people will always be coming in. The religious man should handle a huge turnover of people, coming through and going away.Then he's really working. But he should not get them hooked on the medicine.[21] Alan Watts

6

My Religious Views: Before and After

Prior to my heroic dose, I'd been the biggest atheist imaginable for as long as I can remember. From a young age, I was never able to put my faith in any organized religion. There were too many contradictions with history, clashes with known science, and in my opinion, traditional religion is the root of many of the cruelest atrocities man has ever committed. In my personal experience, many of the meanest, most degrading words ever said to me, we're uttered by people who thumbed the Bible hardest and attended church numerous times per week. Throughout the years, I've kept my thoughts to myself if I thought they may upset someone else's world view. Regardless of their religious affiliation, I've always tried to give everyone an equal chance to show me they were a good person. Many times I've been blown away by how proud some of these people could be in telling me I was in some way, a lesser person than them due to my lack of religious beliefs.

Though I don't believe in any specific 2,000 year old ideologies, I've always been interested in religion for the role it's played throughout history. At this point in time, no single religion has it completely figured out regardless of the certainty they each like to claim. We have some factual historic and geographic information to go by, of course, but nothing that would serve as definitive proof in favor of one over the next. Many of today's popular religions have common themes, dates, stories, and traditions that were started by civilizations that pre-date them by thousands of years.

For instance, it's always been impossible for me to take the story of Noah's Ark literally. In this Christian based myth, a 500 year old man, builds a boat half the size of the Titanic, and put's two of every animal on board during a global flood. We know our average life expectancy is higher today than ever, but we max out around 100 years old. Up until around 1900, life expectancy was less than 60 years old. We also have no record of a boat the size of the Ark being successfully built until the late 1800s. It becomes even harder to take this story as true, once you've read the *Epic of Gilgamesh*. One quickly sees a similar, earlier version of the Noah story, yet this same tale had been recorded thousands of years prior in ancient Sumer. Not only that, but they're countless other flood myths, from Africa to North America, to Asia, to even Australia. How can 49 percent of American Christians claim the Bible is the literal word of god, when in the very first chapter they've plagiarized an ancient story? If one reads the Bible and compares it with other religions and known history, it becomes easy to see that Christianity was created from many ancient pagan traditions and cultures. The Romans were known to adopt other cultures, such as those of the Celts and Greeks in a process known as religious syncretism. This involves the intermingling of two or more religions into a similar or new religion. Buddha, Krishna in Hinduism, Horus in Egyptian Mythology, Dionysus in Greece, and Mithra in Persia, amongst various others, each have similar traits to Jesus, yet were all written hundreds or thousands of years prior. The flood myths, afterlife story, and tree of life, are all areas of Christianity that share common ideas with past spiritual traditions.

Noah's story has the feeling of being far-fetched and exaggerated compared to the known facts of our physical world from the start, but it's very plausible to imagine men simply attempting to save their farm animals during a flash flood or tsunami on any part of the globe at a given time. When you hear a similar story repeated by various groups of people all over the world, it usually means that there's something more to it. An event most likely took place, but was recorded slightly differently by each civilization. Depending on their culture, beliefs, location, and language. The early stories changed over time, much like the children's game known as "telephone." In the same way, various holy sacraments have been consumed by ancient peoples, all over the world in an attempt to communicate with a divine power. As with the flood myths, their descriptions may differ slightly, but the overall message is essentially the same. According to many historical records, all across the globe, there was once some type of plant based food or liquid psychedelic mixture, which once taken, offered the ability to look inside the mind of God.

Even after being a long time non-believer in traditional religion, my psilocybin encounter made me take a step back and reconsider what I believed. I would never attempt to convince others that what I came away feeling towards religion was more correct than anyone else's personal beliefs. From my mushroom experience, I now completely believe there's some form of greater intelligence out there that we don't fully understand. I returned from my hero dose and immediately knew that what I'd felt was where religion came from at its very core. Stories of an afterlife, or heaven and hell make much more sense to me as I can imagine my spirit, or soul, becoming part of the enormous glowing energy mass I met via the mushrooms. I felt that it loved and cared for me, much as followers of Christianity say about Jesus. I also had the overwhelming sense that only the "good" energy would be allowed to get into this place.

I feel certain that most of the world's major ideologies today were created to describe, or enhanced by various psychoactive plants, and mushrooms specifically. I believe that most religions were created after realizing this other realm existed used the primitive language and knowledge of their time to make sense of this almost unfathomable experience, in the best way they could.

I still don't know what to call it, or how to describe it fully - but while I was there, something kept telling me *"Everything is going to be alright."* and then again, a few seconds later *"Everything is going to be alright."* The song, *Three Little Birds* by Bob Marley and *Instant Karma* by John Lennon both have that phrase as a partial lyrics. *"Don't worry, about a thing, cause everything little thing is gonna be alright."* and *"Don't you know it's gonna be alright."* Though Marley isn't known to have taken psychedelics, it's interesting to me that so many of the 60's and 70's largest cultural icons would have that very phrase in their lyrics. It's almost if they were both prophets, spreading the true gospel of peace and love.

As witnessed in both Timothy Leary's Good Friday Experiment and more recently through the research completed at Johns Hopkins, we now know the use of psilocybin can help to facilitate a spiritual experience. Throughout human history, many civilizations have found the keys to spirituality, immortality, and knowledge through a drinkable plant based consciousness. Unfortunately for history's sake, we've never been able to conclude officially, which ingredients were used to unlock these specific secrets. Much of the information we know through literature, suggests that various forms of psychoactive mushrooms are strong candidates to have played a large role in ancient religious traditions.

If you told a random stranger that you took mushrooms, saw the inner workings of the universe, and was in the presence of all knowing loving entity, most people would say you were crazy. In the United States, approximately 80% of the population still follow a major religion, yet a substance that is known to produce life changing spiritual experiences is currently illegal and listed as the most harmful of drugs.

As with politics, many have trouble seeing negative aspects of the groups they affiliate. Today, the most dominate religions focus more on social issues, disputes in past history, and remaining in power than using their influence and message to better the world. Many great people and organizations do positive work in the name of various gods, and that's not a bad thing, but the negative aspects of today's religion overwhelm any positive work done many times over. The problem lies at the heart of these traditional religions. They tell followers that they know the answers to questions we haven't yet discovered as a species and for the most part, anyone who disagrees with these ancient ideas are considered slightly behind the curve.

If what I experienced was truly the same as those written about throughout history, then many followers of today's most popular religions have their priorities completely incorrect. Once one follows the ideals of any specific ideology, they lose some ability to see the world outside of those pre-filtered glasses. I went in without any blinders or ideologies. I know what I saw, believe it to be real and the medical and historical data we have agree there may be something more to it. Overall, as a curious person, my encounter's left me with even more questions than I had before. I don't have all the answers by any means, but I feel that every religion, at their formation, was trying to describe this psychedelic induced world and the understanding that comes with it. The most basic explanation is to simply be kind to others and appreciate what you see around you. Versions of the Golden Rule have been documented during the origins of nearly every major religion. *"Do to others as you would have them do to you"* is the cornerstone of empathy and communal understanding. On my large dose trip, I saw a golden energy of love, that I believe was the same entity which gave this vital information to early man. Religion has been crucial throughout history in attempting to keep this core value alive, especially when times appear darkest. The problem is the message has been over complicated, manipulated, and abused to a point where many times it divides us, instead of making us feel as one. When countries, civilizations, groups, religions or even individuals forget the Golden Rule for periods of time, as a species we tend revert back to using more animalistic tendencies towards others. The remembrance of empathy helps create peace and progress, but can easily be destroyed by those who don't. Good and evil is essentially having empathy opposed to not.

Terence McKenna once asked the mushroom, "*Why us? Why should we be the ambassadors of an alien species into human culture?*" And it replied, "*Because you did not believe in anything. Because you have never given over your belief to anyone.*" [66] Based on my encounter, I came away with a similar feeling. While psilocybin can impact even the most close-minded of individuals in a positive way, I firmly believe the mushroom entity only reveals its deepest secrets to those who keep an open mind and have a true thirst for knowledge.

7

Entheogens as The Tree of Life

The first recorded mention of mushrooms can be found in the form of African cave art, dating back over 10,000 years to 9,000 BCE.[22] Within a short time, Siberian shamans used mushrooms both for medicinal and spiritual purposes. This shows that mushroom use was prevalent in parts of the world for at least 6,000 years before writing was invented in ancient Sumer sometime around 3,200 BCE. We've only been writing for approximately 5,200 years, meaning more time's passed between the earliest cave painting depicting mushrooms and the beginning of written history than from the beginning of written history until today.

R. Gordon Wasson was one of the first Westerners to experience magic mushrooms, and he subsequently wrote about them for Life Magazine. Not ironically, within ten years, he'd published a book titled *Soma: Divine Mushroom of Immortality,* where Wasson claimed the *Amanita muscaria* was the true sacred Soma described in the Rigveda of Hinduism. These mushrooms, commonly seen as bright red with white spots, are also known as *fly agaric*. They contain the psychoactive substances muscimol and ibotenic acid instead of psilocybin. *Amanita muscaria* was used as an entheogen by early indigenous tribes of Siberia and Finland. It was taken both recreationally and as a religious sacrament by the shamans of these arctic regions.[23] In Eastern Siberia, the shaman ate the mushrooms, while the other members of society drank his urine. This essentially allowed the shaman's body to work as a filter, allowing the remaining individuals to consume a more potent version of the substance, without many of the uneasy feelings commonly seen when *Amanita's* are eaten straight from the ground..

Interestingly enough, *Amanita muscaria* mushrooms don't produce nearly the psychedelic effects that psilocybin containing mushrooms do for most who try them. Many claim that *Amanita* only produces a sleepy drunken feeling, with little to no hallucinations. Often users report having strange, extemely vivid dreams after taking them. The strength of these mushrooms varies widely from location to location, as well as seasonally. *Amanitas* found early in the year (spring or summer) have been documented to contain up to ten times more muscimol than those found winter months. It's also been noted that mushrooms that see heavy rain while in a mature state tend to have some of their potentcy washed away compared to those that come to maturity in a dry environment.[71] Even with the reputation of being only mildly psychoactive, some individuals who consume *Amanita muscaria* in today's times report having a trip that closely resembles the psilocybin mushroom experience.

It's thought by many that the story of Santa Claus may have initially originated from these traditions of red-and-white mushroom eating. Fly agaric has a symbiotic relationship with coniferous trees, which causes them to sprout out from under pines, much like presents under the Christmas tree. Shamans would pick these mushrooms and place them upon tree branches, like ornaments, to better allow the sun to dry them out. Reindeers, which are a staple of Siberia, are also known to ingest *Amanita muscaria* and have been recorded digging them out from under the snow in winter. During colder months when snow was prominent, the front entrances of the local tribes' homes were often blocked and impossible to enter. In this case, the shaman would enter the home via the chimney or smoke stack to provide gifts of *Amanita* mushrooms to those inside.[24]

Wasson compared ancient *Amanita*-based traditions from shamans in Siberia to those seen involving the Soma of India. As a result, he found numerous similarities, and the exploration into mushrooms as the possible origin in early religion began.

As the blood of animals and the sap of plants, Soma courses through all living things. He is Inspiration to those who seek it, and so is the god of poets. He is also the god of the moon. He is the dwelling place of the venerated dead, as well as the divine cure for evil.[25]

Lord Soma was a Hindu god residing in the form of a plant. By drinking the juices of this still unknown species of hallucinatory plant, mortals could for a short time see into the realm of gods. Drinking Soma was also reported to reduce fear before battle, inspire artists, and bring about euphoric feelings. The Veda also refers to Soma as Amrita, meaning immortality. In Greek mythology, the gods consumed a beverage known as *nectar* that would give them immortality. Nectar was made from the juices of ambrosia, and referred to as *"food of the gods."* Described as a rosy-red color, the nectar of the ambrosia also highly resembles the characteristics of the Indian Soma of the Rigveda. Amrita, Soma, nectar, and ambrosia can each be used to describe what appears to be the same ancient drink, which was said to provide immortality and inspiration. Scholar Ralph T.H. Griffith translated the followed passage from the Rigveda, which describes the use of Soma:

We have drunk Soma and become immortal; we have attained the light, the Gods discovered. Now what may foeman's malice do to harm us? What, O Immortal, mortal man's deception?

In another Soma-based theory, Albert Hofmann hypothesized that the barley in these areas had been contaminated by a strain of ergot, which resulted in a psychedelic drink, possibly a form of beer.[26] Ergot, otherwise known as *Claviceps,* is a species of fungi that grows on rye, barley, and wheat, and that resemble tiny mushrooms. Ergot contains ergotamine, from which Hofmann first synthesized lysergic acid and eventually LSD, back in 1938. In its natural form though, ergot causes extreme sickness and convulsions and is often deadly. Throughout the Middle

Ages, many towns saw large scale instances of ergot poisoning that were later known as St. Anthony's Fire.

Approximately 10,000 to 13,000 years ago, various grains became some of the first plants to be cultivated through agriculture. Rye, wheat, and barley soon became common in civilizations from Africa, Middle East, and Asia. Ergot can spread rapidly in the correct environments. In 1995, *Claviceps africana* was seen outside of Africa and Asia for the first time after it was located in Brazil. Within three years' time, the ergot had spread throughout South America, into Mexico, and was seen across the Great Plains of the United States. Ergot is most prevalent at average temperatures between 65–75 degrees with close to 100 percent humidity.[27] If temperatures overnight are correct, *Claviceps* can still be found in hot, dry climates as well. Similar to mushrooms, when the conditions are right and spores are nearby, ergot can spread almost anywhere, quickly.

In the book *The Road to Eleusis: Unveiling the Secret of the Mysteries,* Wasson suggests the Eleusinian Mysteries, a secret religious ceremony in ancient Greece, involved the use of ergot-infected grains. Participates would travel to Eleusis, Greece to celebrate the Homeric myth of Demeter and Persephone. In the tale, Demeter, was said to have been the first to learn the secrets of agriculture. Part of the ceremony consisted of an all-night feast that included dancing in the Rharian Field, the spot where humanity grew its first grain. Later in the evening a cow would also be sacrificed. These ceremonies were considered a pilgrimage for the ancient Greeks. From approximately 1,500 BCE to 400 CE, thousands traveled to Eleusis each September for nearly 2,000 years.[28] Each individual was allowed to partake once in their life and swore to keep the initiation rites secret. This was taken very seriously as the punishment for revealing the secrets was death. Individuals would drink an unknown liquid called *Kykeon* and experience unique visions, which had the same familiar traits as nectar and Soma. A participant in the ceremony, Aristides the Rhetor, left us this description:

Eleusis is a shrine common to the whole earth, and of all the divine things that exist among men, it is both the most awesome and the most luminous. At what place in the world have more miraculous tidings been sung, and where have the dromena called forth greater emotion, where has there been greater rivalry between seeing and hearing? [29]

Terence McKenna would later hypothesize psilocybin mushrooms as a possible entheogenic source of both Soma and the Eleusinian Mysteries. He also believed this was the initial reason cows were worshipped in India.[30] In *Food of the Gods*, McKenna explains how the ninth Mandala of the Rigveda mentions the cow as a representation of Soma numerous times. Partially recorded recipes for the drink have said to mix cow's milk with the juice of Soma. If true, this means cattle would have been closely linked to the drink during its preparation. Psilocybin mushrooms, which grow in cow manure and produce similar effects to Soma, then become even more plausible as the key ingredient. Soma was sometimes referred to as having yellow stalks or even greenish features, but were also considered to be "bright shining" in most literature. The same has been said about certain species of psilocybin containing mushrooms.

The cultural-historical meaning of the Eleusinian Mysteries, their influence on European intellectual history, can scarcely be overestimated. Here suffering humankind found a cure for its rational, objective, cleft intellect, in a mystical totality experience that let it believe in immortality, in an everlasting existence. This belief had survived in early Christianity, although with other symbols.[28] Albert Hofmann

The Eleusinian Mysteries were a later version of earlier Greek traditions called the Dionysian Mysteries. The Dionysus cult was an ancient wine cult that based many of their traditions on the life cycle of the grapevine. Upon fermentation, the drinking of the wine was said to make an individual become one with the god's spirit. In time, honey, beeswax, ivy, and various other substances would be added to the drink. Along with wine, beer would be also consumed by later generations.

Following the torches as they dipped and swayed in the darkness, they climbed mountain paths with head thrown back and eyes glazed, dancing to the beat of the drum which stirred their blood.... In the state of ekstasis or enqousiasmos, they abandoned themselves, dancing wildly.... and calling 'Euoi!' At that moment of intense rapture they became identified with the god himself.... They became filled with his spirit and acquired divine powers.[31] Peter Hoyle

Greek wine is known to have been low in alcohol content, suggesting that some of the added mixtures may have played a larger role in these early drinks. Author Robert Graves first suggested this in his book *The Greek Myths*, saying the Dionysians *"used these brews to wash down mouthfuls of a far stronger drug: namely a raw mushroom, Amanita muscaria, which induces hallucinations, senseless rioting, prophetic sight, erotic energy, and remarkable muscular strength."*[32] He would later come to believe psilocybin mushrooms should be considered as a possible source as well. Other psychoactive plants that may have been included by the early Dionysian cults are belladonna, *Datura,* or even cannabis.

As with other early religions, Judaism also had similar traditions involving entheogens. The Essenes were a sect of Judaism who were prevalent from 200 BCE to 100 CE. Though it's officially unknown, they're considered the group most likely to have written the Dead Sea Scrolls. They were advocates for peace and wise from their study of ancient writings. The Essenes lived in communities where all material items were shared and they believed their souls to be immortal. Anyone willing to live a pure life, free of lies and crime, who had the goodness of humanity in their hearts, could join through initiation. They claimed to be keepers of secret knowledge and knew how to communicate with the divine. In order to keep their records safe from the Romans, the Essenes hid their scrolls in caves, where they wouldn't be seen again until they were rediscovered in 1946.

They were the light which shines in the darkness and which invites the darkness to change itself into light. Thus, for them, when a candidate asked to be admitted to their School, it meant that, within him, a whole process of awakening of the soul was set in motion. Such a soul was ready to climb the stairs of the sacred temple of humanity. The Essenes differentiated between the souls which were sleeping, drowsy, and awakened. Their task was to help, to comfort, and to relieve the sleeping souls, to try to awaken the drowsy souls, and to welcome and guide the awakened souls. Only the souls considered as awakened could be initiated into the mysteries of the Brotherhood-Sisterhood.[33] Allison Sledge, *The Quintessential Jesus of Nazareth*

The rapid growth of Christianity resulted in the end of the Greek mysteries and led to the persecution of the Essenes. Though early Christian church leaders banned most traditional Greek customs, many of these rituals played a large role in forming the version of Christianity we see today.

The Hebrew Bible speaks of a substance called *manna,* which may have been psychedelic as well. Manna was a small, white, flaky material that was found on the ground overnight and would melt under the sun's heat by afternoon. If collected and not consumed in a short time, manna would begin to decompose and smell. To better preserve the substance, it was often baked into cakes or bread. Terence McKenna believed heavenly manna resembled the characteristics of *Psilocybe cubensis* mushrooms,[30] while others believe it may have been used to describe *Amanita muscaria.*

Jesus describes the Mannas in detail in the book of John. In this story Jesus attempts to make clear; of manna, there are two different ones/kinds. He describes the manna that he is giving the disciples (last supper) as the Manna that bestows immortality. His statement, unless you have eaten his flesh/body (Soma/Manna), and drink of his blood (Soma Juice), you have no life in you, takes on a whole new meaning in light of this discovery.[24] James Arthur, *Mushrooms and Mankind*

Our fathers did eat manna in the desert; as it is written, He gave them bread from heaven to eat. Then Jesus said unto them, verily. I say unto you, Moses gave you not that bread from heaven; but my father giveth you the true bread from heaven... Then said they unto him, Lord, evermore give us this bread. And Jesus said unto them, I am the bread of life ... The Jews then murmured at him, because he said, I am the bread that came down from heaven.[34] John 6:31-41

In *The Sacred Mushroom and the Cross,* scholar John Marco Allegro wrote that Christianity itself began as a fertility cult that ingested *Amanita muscaria* to understand the mind of God. Allegro was the only agnostic originally sent to translate the Dead Sea Scrolls. By following many words and various languages back to their ancient origin, mostly Sumer and parts of Siberia, Allegro believed that earlier mushroom and cattle cults, under the influence of fly agaric, were where the roots of Christianity began.[35] Through his research, he believed Jesus wasn't a real man, but was more of a secret code for the psychedelic mushroom. Due to the nature of his claims, the book is one of the most controversial of all time. Though *The Sacred Mushroom and the Cross* can be a tough read at times, it's filled with many interesting ideas and it's highly recommended to anyone interested in the role of mushrooms in religion. The introduction contains one of my favorite quotes:

He will allow just a very few of his chosen mortals to share his divinity, it is but for a fleeting moment. Under very special circumstances, he will permit men to rise to the throne of heaven and glimpse the beauty and the glory of omniscience and omnipotence. For those who are so privileged there has seemed no greater or more worthwhile experience. The colors are brighter, the sounds more penetrating, every sensation is magnified, every natural force exaggerated.

In a weird turn of events, R. Gordon Wasson would spend many years attempting to discredit Allegro.[36] Wasson, various Biblical scholars, and the Church itself each took aim at Allegro's seemingly far-out story. Years later, after claiming Allegro's book completely false, Wasson admitted to having never actually read the book.

I once said that there was no mushroom in the Bible. I was wrong. It plays a major hidden role (that is, hidden from us until now) in the best-known episode of the Old Testament, tale of Adam and Eve and the Garden of Eden. I suppose that few at first, or perhaps none, will agree with me. To propose a novel reading of this celebrated story is a daring thing: it is exhilarating and intimidating. I am confident, ready for the storm. R. Gordon Wasson

The cup Jesus was said to have drunk from during the Last Supper is called the Holy Grail. The same cup was then allegedly used by Joseph of Arimathea to catch the blood of Christ while on the cross. Drinking from the Holy Grail is said to provide immortality, much like the secret psychedelic potions of the past. As an *Amanita muscaria* mushroom grows, the fully developed cap will create a bowl, or cup shape. When dew or rainwater collect inside this bright red cap, it turns the liquid inside red as well. As with Soma and others, drinking from these caps would essentially be consuming the blood of Christ from the Holy Grail. If Jesus was really hidden code for the mushroom as Allegro hypothesized, then the *Amanita* truly turns water into wine, as was said about Jesus. The Christian Holy Communion, or Eucharist, involves the consumption of bread and wine, similar to the rituals of the Eleusinian and Dionysian Mysteries. Could it be that ergot-based bread, psychedelic wine, or fly agaric were also involved in the story of the Last Supper?

For I received from the Lord what I also delivered to you, that the Lord Jesus on the night when he was betrayed took bread, and when he had given thanks, he broke it, and said, "This is my body which is for you. Do this in remembrance of me."[34] 1 Corinthians 11:23-24

Is this a hidden clue, left to tell us of a special bread that can help us see the essence of God? The Aztecs called psilocybin mushrooms Teonanacatl, meaning "Divine Flesh," and are sometimes referred to as the "flesh of the Gods." Many of the ancient spiritual sacraments such as nectar were similarly called "food of the Gods."

It's been long repeated that the forbidden fruit eaten from the Tree of Knowledge in the Garden of Eden was an apple. Further research has shown the fruit would have more than likely been an apricot, if not an entheogen.[37] After consuming the fruit, Adam and Eve were given the ability to judge right from wrong. While many believe the Tree of Knowledge and the Tree of Life to be two separate species of plant, some theologians such as Karl Budde theorize that they are one and the same. Regardless, we can still see a Christian reference to gaining wisdom and immortality by eating something from a tree. This story is a recurring theme in almost every major religion.

And the LORD God said, Behold, the man is become as one of us, to know good and evil: and now, lest he put forth his hand, and take also of the tree of life, and eat, and live forever.[34] Genesis 3:22

The tree of golden apples in ancient Norse mythology provided the gods with immortality, much like ambrosia does in Greek mythology. If we take Allegro and McKenna's mushroom-based theories on the subject temporarily out of the equation, the apricot was the most abundant fruit in the area thought to be Eden. Apricots are also referred to as golden apples in some parts of the world. Ancient Chinese mythology contains a story called *"The Peaches of Immortality,"* which shows many similarities to Soma and ambrosia. Peaches are a combination of orange and red, much how the fly agaric mushroom can vary between the two colors. The legend promises immortality and longevity to those who consume it, similar to the ancient Greeks, Indians, and Eleusians. The story also speaks of a dragon, much like the serpent in the Garden of Eden.[38] Greek mythology contains a tree bearing golden apples as well. In the Garden of the Hesperides, these apples were also said to have been guarded by a dragon. In this tale, a goddess similar to Eve enters the garden, gets past the dragon, and illegally picks an apple.[39]

In Islam, the Qur'an also speaks of a "Tree of Immortality." In a similar story to the Christian version, Adam and Eve are tempted by a serpent to eat from the tree. The Baha'i faith also has a tree of life story depicting good versus evil, where males were created from the tree's branches and women from its leaves. In another version, the Baha'i say the roots and trunk are God, the branches devoted followers, and the fruit meant to nourish the growth of civilization.[40] Persian myth speaks of yet another Soma-like plant deity, Haoma. Though described slightly different from the others, as golden green with branches and roots, this plant is also good for the soul and mind, and helps in healing. The sap from Haoma was also coincidentally thought to provide immortality and allowed one person to look inside the mind of another.[41] Ancient Babylon had a similar story where eating the fruit from the Ea Tree was said to provide eternal life. In this tale, much like in the Genesis story, the god of wisdom, Ea, creates the first man, Adapa, with intelligence, but he was still mortal. The god Anu offers Adapa immortality by eating certain foods, but he's tricked by Ea into refusing this power.[42]

In Egyptian mythology, the acacia tree was considered the Tree of Knowledge. Isis and Osiris were said to have been born from under the "*tree in which life and death are enclosed.*" The *Acacia nilotica* grows abundantly along the Nile River and contains a high amount of Dimethyltryptamine. Known as DMT, this is the same psychedelic ingredient that's found in the ayahuasca brews of South America. Freemasons also spoke of the *Acacia nilotica's* importance, which they claim were learned from the ancient Egyptians.[43] The acacia tree could have even been used as a sacrament in Africa, the Middle East, and even in India. Similar to the fly agaric, numerous entheogenic theories involve DMT as the source of both the Haoma and Soma. DMT is essentially psilocybin that's not orally active. The body has the ability to break down dimethyltryptamine quickly via enzymes in the liver called monoamine oxidase. In order to get the psychedelic effects of DMT orally, one must also consume a monoamine oxidase inhibitor (MAOI). With ayahuasca, DMT is found in the leaves of the chacruna or chaliponga plants, while the *Banisteriopsis caapi* vine acts as the MAOI. Any culture attempting to see the effects of the DMT containing *Acacia nilotica* tree would also need to find a MAOI to mix it with. Many believe this was accomplished with the plant *Peganum harmala,* better known as Syrian rue. Syrian rue grew commonly throughout the Middle East and was drought resistant, which would have provided a reliable source for an MAOI. This could mean the Egyptians or surrounding cultures may have had their own secret desert version of ayahuasca. Even today, consuming Syrian rue prior to taking psilocybin mushrooms will enhance the effects as much as double. It's possible that MAOIs may have been added to many of the psychedelic mixtures mentioned in this chapter.

The similarities make it appear as if the legends of a single group were translated, spread, and adopted all over the globe. These early customs would have been shared by word of mouth for hundreds, if not thousands, of years before the final story was documented in each culture. This would account for slightly altered versions of the seemingly same substances and experiences throughout history. The appearance, shape, and effects of both psilocybin and fly agaric mushrooms can vary greatly between species and geographic location. It's possible that the secrets of psychoactive plants in Europe, for instance, made it to Asia, where the description no longer matched an indigenous species. Since we often see religious groups have the same general experiences, whether on ergot beer or bread, fly agaric, psilocybin, or DMT mixtures, it appears as though many different types of plants and fungi allowed access into the same sacred realm. This can still be seen today, as most psychedelic entheogens are known to produce similar experiences.

The Tree of Life was a Babylonian concept, and as represented in carvings it does not look particularly like a tree at all. It was shown as a series of leafy rosettes, arranged and construction in a strange [lattice] pattern... To the Babylonians, it was a tree with magical fruit, which could only be picked by the gods. Dire consequences befell any mortal who dared to pluck from it. The tree found its way into the Hebrew legend of Adam and Eve... which is heavily loaded with allusions of the Ancient of Days.[44] George Sassoon and Rodney Dale, *The Manna Machine*

Tantalus, a figure in Greek mythology, was punished for stealing nectar and ambrosia during a dinner with Zeus on Mt. Olympus. Depending on interpretation, upon his return, he either gave the stolen ambrosia to mortals (commoners) or repeated the secrets he overheard between gods to mortals. Regardless, we have a situation in which the gods don't wish for the average person to have access to their knowledge. Though the gods would let Tantalus off lightly for this crime, he committed a far more serious one when he killed his son and attempted to serve him to the gods during a meal. His punishment was to spend eternity just out of reach of both food and water, where the trees would raise their limbs too high for him to grab the fruit and the water would reside just before he could drink.[45]

It's important to remember that as with the Bible, some Greek myths may represent historical events, but many stories were created to teach lessons and provide warnings. They were often written by the very men working to define right from wrong in their society. The story of Tantalus reinforces two points: There's a terrible punishment awaiting those who commit murder, and more importantly to our story, commoners are not allowed to know the secrets of the gods. If these secrets were truly being guarded by those in the know, stories like this would help to discourage the general population from attempting to learn more.

The ability—or at least impression—that one can speak with the divine is a very valuable asset, even in today's times. The leaders of the early churches would have soon realized this as well. Over time, the drinks of the gods were taken only by the highest members of society. Instead of common folk having their own personal spiritual experience, in which the entire community would participate and grow to understand, eventually, high priests, philosophers, and nobles would be the only ones privy to this information. The interpretations of the remaining few in the know would become sought after by the masses. Instead of having an enlightening, empathetic oneness with those in their community, the majority of society now waited to be told what God thinks and feels by the most powerful men among them. Inevitably, it became more beneficial for those in control to speak towards their personal, political, or social interests than relay their wisdom from encounters on entheogens. As a result of this, elixirs were no longer needed or taken. Many of their secrets were lost outside the few remaining isolated groups that continued to consume them. The written wisdom of the past, which had been backed by these substances, became simply ancient words left to interpretation and twisted by those in power for thousands of years.

While it appears obvious that entheogens, particularly mushrooms, played a large role in the formation of early religion, each of the instances mentioned in this chapter are highly contestable and none are considered to be a clear-cut fact. These are usually considered minority opinions and lack conclusive evidence. There is, however, overwhelming historical evidence that there were plant-based drinks that produced euphoric visions and thoughts of immortality, which were often tied to divinity. The same general entheogenic events were taking place from Europe to Asia for thousands of years before our written history began. Each culture had their own way of creating, administering, and describing their psychoactive drinks, while still attaining and reporting similar results. Entheogens have been taken for thousands of years and mushrooms have been depicted in religious art throughout history. Modern research from two of the top universities in the country, Harvard, in the '60s, and Johns Hopkins ,recently, have produced valid studies documenting psilocybin and other psychedelics effect on religious experience. There's no doubt in my mind that the two are connected. Dr.

Anthony Bossis, PhD of NYU best describes what he's heard from his patients after witnessing many psilocybin-based spiritual encounters:

These concepts form the basis for so many religions: Christ-consciousness, Buddha-nature, Samadi in Hindu, Satori in Zen... There's all this overlap. They speak the words of the mystics without ever having read them.[8]

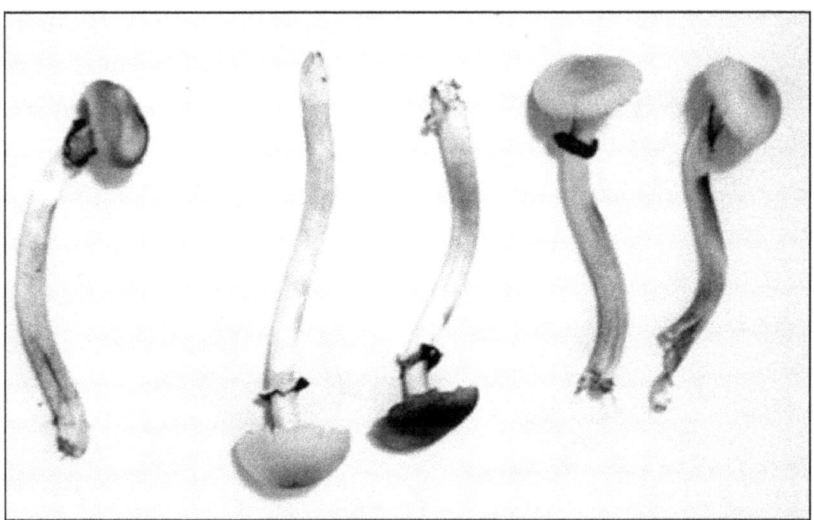

Psilocybe Cubensis (Psilocybin Mushroom)

Ergot Infection on Rye

Acacia Tree (Egypt)

Amanita Muscaria or "Fly Aragic"

Amanita as the Tree of Life in St. Michael's Church, Germany 1192 AD

8

2,000+ Years of Entheogen Suppression

Without psychedelics as a guiding force, the Romans slowly moved away from the ancient Greek philosophies based on rational thought, humanism and science. In time, they would begin to condone almost anyone attempting to understand science because many believed that common man couldn't possibly comprehend the mind of God. As the Roman Empire became the world's most powerful civilization, Local customs and traditions were intertwined into Christianity along the way, but for the most part, paganism, secularism, and science became enemies of the Church.

St. Augustine abused Greek philosophy and called Plato "a fool". He labeled philosophers as "arrogant" and, in line with the New Testament, he taught that "it is the ignorant who enter heaven." Augustine believed that the Fall (of Adam and Eve) corrupted humankind to the extend where they are incapable of using their independent reason to discover the truth. To Augustine, if God wanted to let humankind know something about the world he would have revealed it unambiguously through his word; if God has chosen not to reveal something, then it means that he does not intend humankind to know. - Paul Tobin, *The Rejection of Pascal's Wager*[46]

It seems that Saint Augustine, like many who trust in blind faith, felt threatened by those who could explain what he didn't understand. This was the general mindset of the Roman elite during this time. For over 300 years, the indoctrination into Christianity, which was now mostly, if not entirely non-psychedelic based, continued to spread across Europe. As they conquered, these Roman Christians would destroy thousands of years of historical records and human knowledge as if it was nothing. It's been said that history is written by the winners. If you destroy everything that doesn't agree with your ideology, for a large portion of society, there's only one side that's ever told. Over a 400 year period, the Christian religion would burn over 2 million texts, erasing more than 2,000 years of man's understanding of the world around him. It's impossible to know exactly what was lost during this time, but there's no doubt it was a devastating blow to humanity.

Christians, wherever and whenever they were in a position to do so, attacked and destroyed the repositories of knowledge, namely books and libraries. In 363-364, the Christian emperor Jovian, ordered the pagan library in Antioch to be burnt. Around the year 372, the Christian emperor Valens (d. 378), as part of his persecution of pagans, ordered the burning of non-Christian books in

Antioch. Then in 391, perhaps the greatest intellectual tragedy of all, the great library of Alexandria (which was reputed to house 700,000 books on all subjects) was destroyed by a group of monks led by Theophilus (d. 412), bishop of Alexandria. Pope Gregory The Great (c. 540-604) was the person responsible for destroying the last collection of older Roman works in the city. Up to the fifth century, many Greco Roman cities had libraries which housed more than 100,000 books. These were all destroyed by the Christians. - Paul Tobin, *The Rejection of Pascal's Wager* [46]

It's not surprising that due to this suppression of knowledge, Europe fell into what's now known as the Dark Ages. For the next 700+ years, the production of non-Christian books and written manuscripts were almost non-existent. Writers and philosophers could not express and share their thoughts freely if they weren't in line with the Church's teachings. They were often punished for proposing new ideas in the fields of science, nature, and medicine. As classical Latin was combined with the languages of newly conquered cultures, in many areas, the few ancient texts available to commoners were not translated fully or understood by the average person of the day.

The Dark Ages have been noted for their backwardness. Far less cultural achievements were accomplished in this time than in the centuries before and after. As Rome rose and fell, sects of Christianity, Islam, and Judaism began to break off and fight each other over whose interpretation of the same basic idea was correct. Anything could be done in the name of religion by those in power and very few commoners had the ability to get a new idea out to the public without being persecuted, tortured, or killed. For centuries, greedy, egotistic rulers built on the atrocities of their predecessors until man had gotten so far away from the philosophical civilizations of the past that humanity's forward progress nearly came to a complete stop. The only sign of mushrooms or entheogens in traditional religions during this time in Europe was seen in the form of Christian art. It appears that even though the majority of Christian civilizations had indeed abandoned psychedelic potions, numerous art exists showing that at least in certain areas, the imagery of the mushroom lived on. In his book, *The Mushroom in Christian Art: The Identity of Jesus in the Development of Christianity,* author John Rush provides over 250 images showing mushroom use in Christian religious art between the second and twelfth centuries CE. Numerous images of Jesus and Mushrooms can be found painted into old world frescos, incorporated in the stained glass of churches, and illustrated in various documents. Rush's work leaves little doubt that for close to 1,000 years, certain aspects of Christianity still held the mushroom sacred. It's thought, both by Rush and John Marco Allegro, that the mushroom was hidden in these works by those in power to help pass the ancient secret of entheogenic powers from one generation to the next.[48]

In the 1330's, Italian philosopher Francesco Petrarca, or Petrarch, who was also known as the Father of Humanism, began to read what was left of the ancient Greek texts from the past. As he learned the works of Seneca and others, Petrarca soon realized that there was a huge difference in society between the time he lived and that of the ancient Greeks and Romans. In the past, they'd been able to discuss and adapt new ways to better their societies, whereas he saw those same attributes being suppressed during his day. Unlike Saint Augustine, Petrarca believed man could make new discoveries in the physical world, while also believing in God. He believed that man was inherently good, with the ability to think for themselves, and not in need of redemption.[49] It appears Petrarca figured this out on his own, mostly on societal differences alone, without actually taking any psychedelics himself. Many believe his humanistic philosophy sparked the end of the Dark Ages, and the beginning of the Italian Renaissance.

Petrarca would read and share the philosophies of the ancient Greeks and Romans with fellow free thinkers of the time, encouraging them to read classic Greek literature. During this period, ancient manuscripts began to be translated from Latin to Greek, allowing more access to a broader portion of the population. As a result, in the early 1400's, starting in Italy, Europe began to see a surge in literature, philosophy, art, music, and science. The word given to this time later by historians, *renaissance* fittingly means "rebirth" or "revival." During this well-known period, we were privileged to the talents of Machiavelli, Dante, Michelangelo, da Vinci, Copernicus, and Galileo, amongst countless others. In reading a vast amount of ancient manuscripts, it would be hard to imagine Petrarca and many others not coming across information on the entheogenic rituals of the past, especially in Eleusis and Dionysis. Two of the greatest minds from this period, Michelangelo and Leonardo da Vinci were both said to have taken the MOAI, *Peganum harmala,* also known as Syrian rue. This is the same plant thought to have been taken with the bark of the Acacia tree in Egypt to form a type of "desert ayahuasca." Each man said taking rue increased their artistic abilities.

Leonardo da Vinci and Michelangelo both claimed that, owing to rue's metaphysical powers, their eyesight and creative inner vision had been improved. Branches of rue were used to sprinkle holy water before High Mass. - Joseph Bruno, *And Now There is Light.*[50]

If two men of that historic stature were taking an entheogen that improves creativity, it would not be surprising if many of the best minds from the time were also turned on to these newly rediscovered plant medicines. Though there was a resurgence in many forms of thinking, knowledge, and art, prominent rulers and traditional religion still had the most power and influence over society. Many great thinkers of this time were jailed, ridiculed, or killed for simply stating ideas we know today to be fact. In time, secular backlash by the majority of believers and a doubling down on popular religion would gradually slow the humanist movement. Most scholars believe the Renaissance period came to an end somewhere between 1600 and 1650.

The same way high levels of religion in the Dark Ages were followed by the Italian Renaissance, high levels of religion seen during the 1950's in the United States were followed by the psychedelic movement of the 60's. Music, art, and humanist ideals again became present. Trip reports from this time, often spoke of the same deep spiritual experiences, first described by the ancients: Peace, Love, and Unity, and Empthy. After having these experiences, much of the youth did want to be involved with the Vietnam War. They also began to fight harder for civil rights and equality. These oppositions to the status quo caused the movement to be radicalized by those in power. The government moved quickly. Within a few years, nearly all psychedelic drugs and psychoactive substances were banned. Unlike the burning of the Library of Alexandria, or the sacking of Rome during the Renaissance, by the 60's technology had made it much harder to completely erase factual history again.

Though still listed as a Schedule 1 drug, psychedelics would then continue to be taken underground for over fifty years since. As science, medicine, and technology have rapidly progressed in the last 20 years, there's been what's called a psychedelic renaissance taking place today. Based on what we know from the past, there's really no better way to describe it.

Throughout history, from Eleusis to Florence to San Francisco, when traditional religion is curtained and psychedelics become involved, philosophy, art, music, science, and humanity have benefited. We've progressed greatly in our understanding of the world during those moments in time. In comparison, the more religious a society has been historically, the fewer new ideas are formed, because many do not think on a level outside the possibilities the religion allows for. The over religious typically spend more time justifying where everything fits in relation to their particular view, rather than taking the best new information and evolving with the times. Ideas that don't agree with biblical or ancient religious text are still often thrown out and criticized, just as they have been for centuries.

To recap, entheogens were used in religious ceremonies for thousands of years. As Rome conquered foreign lands, they spread Christianity, which early on abandoned psychedelic plants. Anything that wasn't in line with their beliefs was destroyed and suppressed for the next 1000 years. In the 1300-1400's, Italians began rereading ancient Greek texts. Within a short time, some of the most famous individuals in history reportedly took the same possible ingredients from 2,000 years ago and had similar experiences. Religion conquered again, but the Founding Fathers of the United States were able to carve a spot for future change. In the 1960's psychedelics returned and were subsequently ridiculed and banned. We're just now beginning to understand these long lost secrets again.

Psilocybin is a source of gnosis, and the voice of gnosis has been silenced in the Western mind for at least a thousand years... Our institutions, our epistemologies are bankrupt and exhausted; we must start anew and hope that with the help of shamanically-inspired personalities, we can cultivate this ancient mystery once again. The Logos can be unleashed, and the voice that spoke to Plato and Parmenides and Heraclitus can speak again in the minds of modern people. - Terence McKenna, *The Archaic Revival*[55]

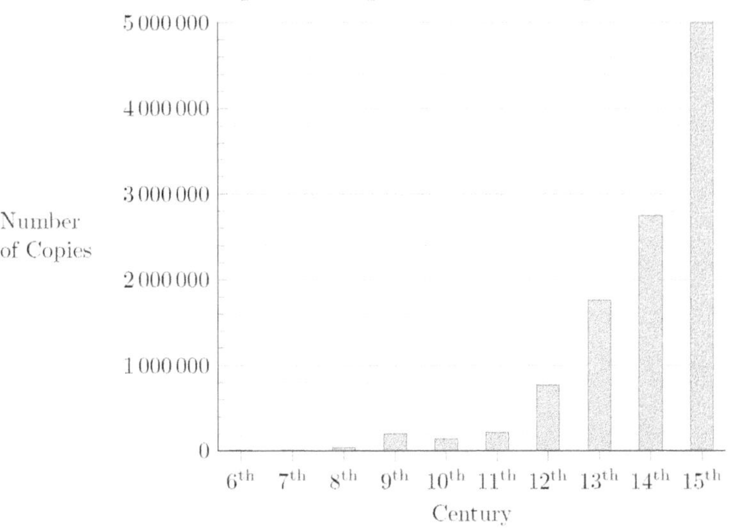

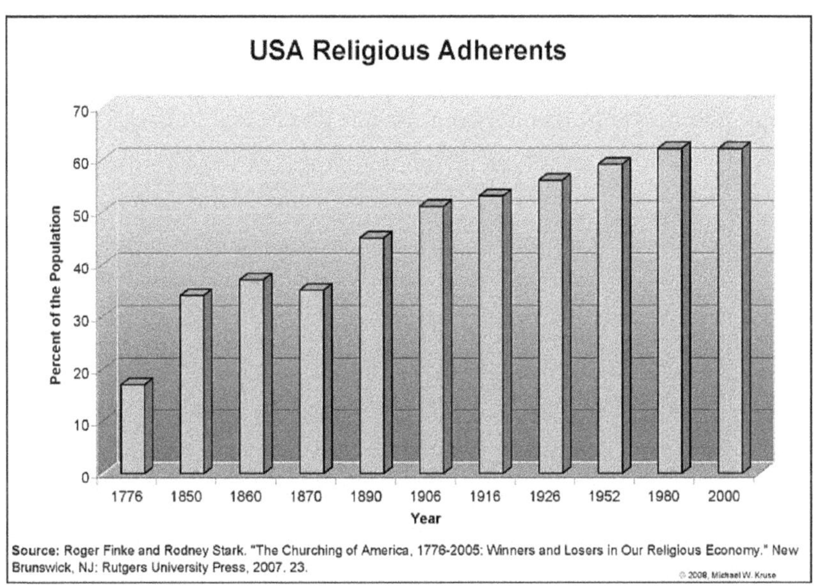

Believe it or not, the USA only had 16% Religious Adherence in 1776.

9

Psychedelics in the Americas

Psilocybin mushrooms and psychedelic entheogens weren't taken only in Eurasia. They also played a large role across the Atlantic in the religious practices of the ancient Americas. After R. Gordon Wasson traveled to Mexico to take psilocybin mushrooms with Marina Sabina, he soon realized many similarities between the description of the effects in the Soma of Hinduism and in his personal experiences. Wasson believed this was not a coincidence, but the adaptation of ancient Siberian shamanic practices that had made their way to the new world early in man's history.[23]

The Olmec civilization lived in Mexico and were predecessors to the ancient Maya and Aztecs. Though other civilizations pre-date them by thousands of years, the Olmec flourished during the same time period as the Eleusinians, between 1,400 BCE to 400 BCE. While there's little written evidence from the Olmecs, artifacts and drawings suggest a strong case for entheogenic use in their culture. The Olmecs were found to have buried *Bufo marinus* toads with their high priests. Many of their sculptures also show men shape shifting into animals, as commonly seen in later Mayan and Aztec artwork.[56] Toads are clearly not entheogens, but one native to the area contained a unique, yet similar substance. In research done on over 285 species of toads, only the *Bufo alvarius,* also known as either the Sonoran Desert toad or the Colorado River toad, contains the psychedelic compound, 5-MeO-DMT. The *Bufo marinus* contains trace amounts of the tryptamine alkaloid, bufotenin. Bufotenin is similar in chemical structure to psilocybin, 5-MeO-DMT, and N,N-DMT. While *Bufo marinus* contains only a very small amount of bufotenin, no psychedelic 5-MeO-DMT has been found in the species.[57]

The Bufo (marinus) toad plays a substantial part in the mythology of the ancient Mesoamerican civilizations of the Olmec, Mayan, and Aztec, and can be found represented in these culture's artwork as far back as 2000BCE. Large quantities of Bufo skeletons have been found at Olmec ceremonial sites. There is some debate over whether or not they were a food source, as certain toxins in their skin are deadly. Some anthropologists have proposed that these toads were used as an entheogen source, and "evidence" for this view comes from toad representations in Aztec art. Many of these descriptions focus in detail on the toads' parotid glands, where the major supply of their venom lies. These include a sculpture in Mexico City's incredible National Museum of Anthropology and a glyph at the palace in Palenque, in which three circles down the toad's back rep-

resent parotid glands. - James Oroc, *Tryptamine Palace. 5-MeO-DMT and the Sonoran Desert Toad* [58]

By looking at maps of where the two species of toads live, we find that most of Mexico and South America's less mountainous regions contain *Bufo marinus,* while the Colorado River toad's habitat is only a small area in the northwest corner of Mexico and into the southwest United States.

The area to which Bufo alvarius is presently native was once inhabited by archaic desert cultures; it is also the putative homeland of the Uto-Aztecans, from which they expanded southward into Mexico as early as 1500 B.C. Was it the shamans of the pre-agricultural desert cultures who discovered the potent psychotomimetic effects of toad poison and whose ecstatic trance experiences gave rise to the now widespread belief in the toad as a transforming shamaness? - Peter Furst, anthropologist[59]

According to Furst and others, it would seem as though the early Olmec migrated directly through the area inhabited by the DMT containing toad before settling in an area with similar, yet non-psychedelic toads. It's plausible that these cultures didn't know the differences between the two species as they are commonly mistaken by even today. They may have worshipped the incorrect toad at times, assuming both species were one and the same. While we are unsure of the use of 5-MeO-DMT in the form of toad venom, there's no doubt that psilocybin mushrooms, ayahuasca, and even Fly Aragic were consumed during rituals by the ancient people in central and South America for thousands of years.

Mushroom stones found in Guatemala, which predate the Spanish, have been dated back to 1,000 BCE.[60] While we have very few written artifacts directly from the Mayan and Aztecs themselves, the Spanish witnessed and described the use of psilocybin mushrooms in the America's in great detail.

Early chroniclers such as Francisco Hernandez, physician to the King of Spain, described several sacred mushroom species. 'Others when eaten cause madness that on occasion is lasting of which the symptom is a kind of uncontrolled laughter. Usually called teyhuintli , these are deep yellow, acrid of a not displeasing freshness. There are others again, which without inducing laughter bring before the eyes all kinds of things such as wars and the likeness of demons. Yet others are not less desired by princes for their fiestas and banquets, of great price. With nightlong vigils they are sought, awesome and terrifying. Richard Evans Schultes[61]

The divine mushroom was taken during ritual ceremonies. Successful Aztec merchants sponsored night banquets. The Florentine Codex records that when the participants ate the mushrooms with honey, and they began to take effect, the Aztecs danced, wept, and saw hallucinations. Others entered their houses in a serious manner and sat nodding. Visions included prophecies of one's own death battle scenes, or war captives that one would take in battle. Others reported visions that they would be rich. All that could possibly happen to a person could be seen under the effects of the mushrooms. After the effect wore off, people would consult among themselves and tell each other about their visions. - Marlene Dobkin de Rio, Ph.d. 62

Mescaline is another type of psychoactive susbstance used in early South American traditions. This psychedelic is most commonly found in San Pedro, Peruvian Torch, and Peyote cacti. Carbon dating tells us that use of the San Pedro was prominent as early as 1,300 BCE, while carvings depicting Peyote can be dated further back in history, to approximately 3,700 BCE. This evidence tells us that on both sides of the Atlantic, the use of psychedelic plants and fungi pre-date written language by thousands of years.

"It is found in the north country. Those who eat or drink it see visions either frightful or laughable. This intoxication lasts two or three days and then ceases. It is a common food of the Chichimeca, for it sustains them and gives them courage to fight and not feel fear nor hunger nor thirst. And they say that it protects them from all danger." Fray Bernardino de Sahagún, 16th century explorer[61]

As with psilocybin mushrooms, little is known about the early use of these substances. Most of what we know today, again comes from the writings made by the Spanish during, or around the Inquisition. Around this time, the use of Peyote was made made illegal and newly converted Christians who were found to have participated in these traditional rituals were charged with heresy. The constant punishment for using psychedelics in central and South America caused those who continued to participate in these ancient practices to go underground, usually deep into the mountains or jungle. An edict issued during this time states, "*The use of the herb or root called peyote… introduced into these Provinces for the purpose of detecting thefts, of divining other happenings and of foretelling future events, it is an act of superstition condemned as opposed to the purity and integrity of our Holy Catholic Faith."*[28]

Ayahuasca was also reported by Spanish missionaries to be used by those indigenous to South and Central America. As with mushrooms, the plant-based drink was considered evil and to be the work of the devil.[63] When ayahuasca was first studied in the twentieth century, the scientists amazingly intended to name the active chemical in the caapi vine *Telepathine* due to its telepathic nature.[64] Users of ayahuasca have reported being able to see the future, communicate with gods, and shapeshift into other entities. They soon discovered that Telepathine was already classified as harmine, the same active compound found in Syrian rue.

As the Romans had more than 1,000 years prior throughout Europe, Spanish conquistadors, such as Hernan Cortes and Francisco Pizarro attempted to eliminate all non-Christian spiritual practices. The majority of Aztec, Mayan, and Incan history was lost forever. With their history destroyed, and death to those who dared to openly continue their use, by the 1600's, mushroom and ayahuasca worship was only practiced in secret. Exactly as happened when the Roman Empire brutally spread their ideology, thousands of years of human history and knowledge were erased by the Spanish over a few hundred years and replaced again, by Christianity. For the most part, the power of the divine mushroom and ayahuasca were practiced only in secret for generations to come and it stayed that way for the next 400 years.

When the Spanish arrived in Mexico in the sixteenth century, they persecuted those priests and practitioners who used the sacred plants in religious rituals. Whatever the visionary effects that informants attributed to the various hallucinogens, these prelates concluded that the devil himself was involved. The Spanish, writing about the effects of the mushrooms, always conjured up the devil, but we shall really never know if the Aztecs were seeing anything like the Christian devil. - Marlene Dobkin de Rio, Ph.D.[62]

The Church of Santo Daime in Brazil was founded in the 1930's and contains a similar message to earlier entheogenic cultures. They combine common Christianity with local ayahuasca rituals. The group preaches truth, love, and justice as its core principles. The drink is called *Daime* meaning give me. Notice how Somaesque key words such as *light, power, truth, love, joy,* and *encountering God* are provided to those who drink ayahuasca. Professor Benny Shannon from the University of Jerusalem translated the following passages from native Portuguese:

"Daime force, Daime light
Daime love!
Daime, the professor of all professors
I have taken this drink
It has incredible power
It demonstrates to all of us
Here in this truth
I have climbed, I have climbed, I have climbed
I have climbed with joy
When reaching the Heights

I encountered the Virgin Mary
I have climbed, I have climbed, I have climbed
I have climbed with love
I have encountered the Eternal Father
And the Redeemer, Jesus Christ"

For centuries the medicinal and spiritual use of entheogens in the Americas was isolated to small groups, villages, and select individuals who kept the ancient traditions alive. Mushrooms would stay hidden from most of the world until anthropologist Robert Weitlaner witnessed a Mezatec mushroom ceremony in the 1930s. Not long after, in 1952, author of *The Greek Myths,* Robert Graves would send R. Gordon Wasson a letter discussing the work of ethnobotanist Richard Evans Schultes on psilocybin mushrooms. Schultes was also the first Westerner to research and describe ayahuasca in scientific journals. Author William Burroughs would read these reports, travel to South America and write what would be known as *The Yage Letters,* along with 60s icon, Allen Ginsberg.

Every tree, every plant, has a spirit. People may say that a plant has no mind. I tell them that a plant is alive and conscious. A plant may not talk, but there is a spirit in it that is conscious, that sees everything, which is the soul of the plant, its essence, what makes it alive. I feel a great sorrow when trees are burned, when the forest is destroyed. I feel sorrow because I know that human beings are doing something very wrong. When one takes ayahuasca one can sometimes hear how the trees cry when they are going to be cut down. They know beforehand, and they cry. – Pablo César Amaringo, retired Peruvian ayahuasquero[65]

Codex Vindobonensis: Mushrooms in Mayan Art

Guatemalan Mushroom Stones

Aztec Mushroom Eaters

Codex Magliabechiano : 16th Century Aztec Art:

Peyote Cactus: Lophophora Williamsii

San Pedro Cactus: Echinopsis pachanoi

Ayahuasca: Psychotria viridis (Chacruna) & Banisteriopsis caapi (vine)

Bufo alvarius: Colorado River Toad

CONCLUSION

To recap, magic mushrooms have been found in artwork and writing on every continent outside Antarctica. Before Christianity dominated the globe, had a special entheogenic drink that allowed them to speak with the divine. Islam, Christianity, Hinduism, Judaism, and even Buddhism all have a sacred Tree of Life from which enlightenment and knowledge was thought to originate from. The documented effects of those ancient substances are very similar to the known experiences of psychedelic plants today. Researchers from one of the best medical schools in the world, Johns Hopkins University, have found that the psilocybin in magic mushrooms induces spiritual experiences. Outside of the Good Friday Experiments, when John Marco Allegro and R. Gordon Wasson wrote their books, we didn't have the medical research we do today. It's time, once and for all to put two and two together. We must begin telling others the truth: Religion was created as a way to describe the experiences of psychedelic plant use by . I believe there's enough information becoming available today for society to collectively take a definitive leap in this direction.

The fact that these substances are illegal today is a crime against humanity, which must be overturned as soon as possible. I personally changed my religious views from an atheist to a deist after my heroic dose, so I'm not saying abandon God. I am saying, however, that traditional religions have their priorities and even history completely wrong. Religion forms a framework which forces their members to limit how they think and act. Morality doesn't have to be enforced by scare tactics any longer.

Looking back, I often wonder if that initial trip with my friend at my apartment may have changed my life forever, just as much (if not more) than my ego-obliterating heroic dose at age thirty did. When I was a carefree kid, in smaller dosages, psilocybin let me see the world in a way I'll never forget. As a stressed adult, frustrated with everyday life, it was somehow able to teach me even more. The mushroom showed me that the world had really never changed; only the way I'd perceived it did.

Without my experiences, I doubt I would have taken a high dose, even if I thought it could help. If I hadn't found that specific amount of mushrooms on the day of my heroic dose, it may have been months or years before I went looking again. If my friend hadn't convinced me that night to take them instead of waiting, I feel my life would be very different today. I've learned so much invaluable information about myself through the ups and downs of the bad years that it would be a shame if I didn't have that knowledge with me today. I could go on, but in the end, as I've said before, it happened exactly as it was supposed to.

We often fall into routines and create patterns to help make sense of our complicated day-to-day life. Sometimes the smallest change in those patterns can send us off track, and almost unknowingly, into a downward spiral. The longer those feelings persist, the harder it can be to pull yourself back up. It can be very difficult to watch close friends continue down that same path without attempting to intervene. I've learned over time that you can't make people change unless they are willing and wanting to. They must have their own true intention to make successful changes or it's unlikely to happen. You could give the best advice and leave it on someone's doorstep, but you can't force them to take it inside. If you know a person who's in this situation, be kind and encouraging, and let them know you care about them. Help them attempt conventional methods of therapy and if those don't work, let them know that more options are available.

Many of the psilocybin studies have shown that the effects seem to wear off slightly over time. While this may be true in certain instances, areas, or individuals, I don't think it's possible for me personally to ever completely go back to the way I was prior. Negative moments can and will occur in life, but I don't get stuck on negative events anymore, the way I did in the past. My cure was taking 55 grams of *Psilocybe cubensis* mushrooms in silent darkness one time. After only four hours, I'd erased many years of self-doubt and regrets and replaced them with the feeling that a stream of endless possibilities awaited me. From the knowledge learned by the extraordinary teams of researchers conducting studies, to my personal experience, I fully believe that psilocybin can help or even cure many anxiety, depression,

OCD, and PTSD related mental health issues safely, and much quicker than traditional methods can.

I've known hundreds of good people who've had both traumatic and smaller events send them into bouts of depression and anxiety, sometimes completely crippling their lives. I've seen pretty girls who won't go out because of their perception of themselves. I've met numerous other individuals who go to certain places only late at night, in order to stay hidden from the world. Many of these people, from an outsider's perspective, look perfectly normal and content, but in their own mind are secretly in a constant state of misery or panic. I've also seen the effects of PTSD and the issues caused by antidepressants first-hand. There is a better way to solve this problem and psychedelics will undoubtedly play a large role in the future. With so many people suffering from these symptoms, we owe it to ourselves as a species to investigate every possible solution. When individuals are again able to consume entheogens without fear of jail or social persecution, the world will undoubtedly become a more peaceful place. Trust me.

My fate is to live among varied and confusing storms. But for you perhaps, if as I hope and wish, you will live long after me. There will follow a better age. This sleep of forgetfulness will not last forever. When the darkness has been dispersed, our descendants can come again in the former pure radiance. Francesco Petrarch

~ Everything is going to be alright ~

References

1. *"Timothy Leary: The Man Who Turned On America."* BBC Documentary, 2001. Online Media.

2. Doblin, Rick. *"Dr. Leary's Concord Prison Experiment: A 34 year follow-up study."* Journal of Psychoactive Drugs; Oct-Dec 1998, Vol. 30, No. 4; ProQuest Medical Library. pg. 419.

3. Doblin, Rick. *Pahnke's "Good Friday Experiment": A long-term follow-up and methodological critique.* The Journal of Transpersonal Psychology, 1991, Vol. 23, No.1.

4. Roberts, Thomas B. *"Recollections of the Good Friday Experiment: An Interview with Houston Smith."* 1 Oct. 1996. Web. 24 Dec. 2014.

5. U.S. Food and Drug Administration. *"FDA Controlled Substance Act."* 30 Dec. 2014. http://www.fda.gov/regulatoryinformation/legislation/ucm148726.htm

6. "*Safety, tolerability, and efficacy of psilocybin in 9 patients with obsessive-compulsive disorder.*" Moreno FA, Wiegand CB, Taitano EK, Delgado PL. J Clin Psychiatry. 2006 Nov;67(11): 1735-40.

7. "*Pilot study of psilocybin treatment for anxiety in patients with advanced-stage cancer.*" Grob CS, Danforth AL, Chopra GS, Hagerty M, McKay CR, Halberstadt AL, Greer GR. Arch Gen Psychiatry. 2011 Jan;68(1):71-8. doi: 10.1001/archgenpsychiatry.2010.116. Epub 2010 Sep 6.

8. Morin, Roc. "*Prescribing Mushrooms for Anxiety.*" The Atlantic. Atlantic Media Company, 22 Apr. 2014. Web. 23 Dec. 2014.

9. New York University. Psychiatry. "*The Potential of Psilocybin to Alleviate Psychological and Spiritual Distress in Cancer Patients Is Revealed. The Potential of Psilocybin to Alleviate Psychological and Spiritual Distress in Cancer Patients Is Revealed.*" N.p., 30 Jan. 2013. Web. 30 Dec. 2014.

10. "*Mystical-type experiences occasioned by psilocybin mediate the attribution of personal meaning and spiritual significance 14 months later.*" Griffiths R, Richards W, Johnson M, McCann U, Jesse R. J Psychopharmacol. 2008 Aug;22. Epub 2008 Jul 1.

11. Zaitchik, Alexander. "*Flashback! Psychedelic Research Returns.*" *Salon.com*. N.p., 28 Sept. 2011. Web. 28 Dec. 2014.

12. Gregoire, Carolyn. "*Could Psychedelics Be An Effective Suicide Prevention Measure?*" The Huffington Post. N.p., 22 Jan. 2015. Web. 23 Jan. 2015.

13. Stamets, Paul. "*Mushrooms of the World: An Indentification Guide.*" (1996), p. 39.

14. "*Studying the effects of classic hallucinogens in the treatment of alcoholism: rationale, methodology, and current research with psilocybin*". Bogenschutz MP. Curr Drug Abuse Rev. 2013 Mar; 6(1):17-29. Review.

15. "*Pilot study of the 5-HT2AR agonist psilocybin in the treatment of tobacco addiction*". Johnson MW, Garcia-Romeu A, Cosimano MP, Griffiths RR.J Psychopharmacol. 2014 Nov 28.Epub 2014 Sep 11.

16. Johns Hopkins University School of Medicine. Psychiatry and Behavioral Sciences. "*'Magic Mushrooms' Help Longtime Smokers 'Quit.*" N.p., 11 Sept. 2014. Web. 23 Dec. 2014.

17. "*The effects of psilocybin and MDMA on between-network resting state functional connectivity in healthy volunteers.*" Roseman L, Leech R, Feilding A, Nutt DJ, Carhart-Harris RL. Front Hum Neurosci. 2014 May 27;8:204. eCollection 2014.

18. Davenport, Francesca. "*New Study Discovers Biological Basis for Magic Mushroom 'Mind Expansion'*" Imperial College London, 3 July 2014. Web. 24 Dec. 2014.

19. "*Effects of psilocybin on hippocampal neurogenesis and extinction of trace fear conditioning*". Briony J. Catlow, Shijie Song, Daniel A. Paredes, Cheryl L. Kirstein and Juan Sanchez-Ramos; *Experimental Brain Research*, published online June 2, 2013.

20. Baier, Anne DeLotto. "*Low Doses of Psychedelic Drug Erases Conditioned Fear in Mice.*" USF Health News. N.p., 15 July 2013. Web. 28 Dec. 2014.

21. Watts, Alan. "*The Use of LSD and Psilocybin*". YouTube. Retrieved 29 Dec. 2014.

22. Myers, Luke A. *Gnostic Visions: Uncovering the Greatest Secret of the Ancient World.* Bloomington, IN: IUniverse, 2011.

23. Wasson, R. Gordon. *Soma: Divine Mushroom of Immortality.* New York: Harcourt, Brace & World, 1968.

24. Arthur, James. *Mushrooms and Mankind: The Impact of Mushrooms on Human Consciousness and Religion.* Escondido, CA: Book Tree, 2000.

25. Henshey, Lori. "*Soma Plant: Portal to the Gods.*" Examiner.com. N.p., 31 July 2011. Web.

26. Hofmann, Albert. *LSD, My Problem Child.* New York: McGraw-Hill, 1980.

27. Isakeit, T., G. N. Odvody, and R. A. Shelby. "*First report of sorghum ergot caused by Claviceps africana in the United States.*" Plant Disease 82.5 (1998): 592-592.

28. Wasson, R. Gordon; Hofmann, Albert; Ruck Carl A. P. *The Road to Eleusis: Unveiling the Secret of the Mysteries.* New York: Harcourt Brace & Jovanovich, 1978.

29. Ruck, Carl A. P. *Sacred Mushrooms: The Secrets of Eleusis.* Berkeley, CA: Ronin, 2006.

30. Mckenna, Terence. *Food of the Gods The Search for the Original Tree of Knowledge A Radical History of Plants, Drugs, and Human Evolution.* New York: Bantam, 1993.

31. Hoyle, Peter. *Delphi.* London: Cassell, 1967.

32. Graves, Robert. *The Greek Myths.* Baltimore: Penguin, 1955.

33. Sledge, Allison. *Quintessential Jesus of Nazareth: An Astrological Interpretation of the Messiah's Natal Chart.* Bloomington, IN: Authorhouse, 2011.

34. "*King James Bible*". Nashville, TN: Holman Bible, 1973.

35. Allegro, John Marco. *The Sacred Mushroom and the Cross; A Study of the Nature and Origins of Christianity within the Fertility Cults of the Ancient Near East.* Garden City, NY: Doubleday, 1970.

36. Irvin, Jan, and Andrew Rutajit. *Astrotheology & Shamanism: Unveiling the Law of Duality in Christianity and Other Religions.* San Diego, CA: Book Tree, 2005.

37. Abrams Akinkuotu, Mary Elizabeth. *Woman in Travail: Travailing for Abraham's Seed.* Bloomington: AuthorHouse, 2009.

38. Anthony C. Yu. *Journey to the West.* University of Chicago Press. 1984.

39. Johnson, Robert Bowie. *Athena and Kain: The True Meaning of Greek Myth.* Annapolis, MD: Solving Light, 2003.

40. Smith, Peter. *Aghsán: A Concise Encyclopedia of the Bahá'í Faith.* Oxford: Oneworld Publications. 2000.

41. Rudgley, Richard. *Encyclopedia of Psychoactive Substances.* London: Abacus, 1999.

42. Mark, Joshua J. "*The Myth of Adapa.*" Ancient History Encyclopedia. N.p., 23 Feb. 2011. Web. 26 Dec. 2014.

43. Christie, Ben. "*The Egyptians Had Their Own Version Of Ayahuasca They Called "The Tree Of Life".*" Collective Evolution. N.p., 31 May 2014. Web. 24 Dec. 2014.

44. Sassoon, George, and Rodney Dale. *The Manna Machine.* London: Sidgwick and Jackson, 1978.

45. "Tantalus". *Encyclopædia Britannica. Encyclopædia Britannica Online.* Encyclopædia Britannica Inc., 2014. Web. 24 Dec. 2014

46. Tobin, Paul. *The Rejection of Pascal's Wager: A Skeptic's Guide to the Bible and the Historical Jesus.* Authors OnLine, 2009.

48. Rush, John A. *The Mushroom in Christian Art: The Identity of Jesus in the Development of Christianity.* Berkeley, CA: North Atlantic, 2011.

49. *Famous First Facts International.* H. W. Wilson Company, New York. 2000.

50. Bruno, Joseph. *And Now There Is Light.* N.p.: Joseph Bruno, 2006.

55. McKenna, Terence. *The Archaic Revival.* New York: HarperCollins, 1991.

56. Kennedy, Alison Bailey. "*Ecce Bufo: the toad in nature and in Olmec iconography.*" Current Anthropology (1982): 273-290.

57. Lever, Christopher. "*The Cane Toad. The history and ecology of a successful colonist.*" Westbury Publishing. 2001.

58. Oroc, James. "*Tryptamine Palace: 5-MeO-DMT and the Sonoran Desert Toad.*" Rochester, VT: Park Street, 2009.

59. Furst, Peter. *Flesh of the Gods: The Ritual Use of Hallucinogens.* New York: Praeger, 1972.

60. De Borhegyi, Carl. "*The Origin of a Mushroom Religion in the Americas.*" MushroomStone.com. N.p., 2010. Web. 24 Dec. 2014.

61. Schultes, Richard Evans, Hoffman, Albert. "*Plants of the Gods: Their Sacred, Healing, and Hallucinogenic Powers.*" Alred van der Marck, New York. 1979.

62. Dobkin de Rios M. "*Hallucinogens: Cross-cultural Perspectives.*" University of New Mexico Press. 1984.

63. Reichel-Dolmatoff, Gerardo. "*The Shaman and the Jaguar: A Study of Narcotic Drugs among the Indians of Colombia.*" Philadelphia: Temple UP, 1975.

64. Luke, D. "*Telepathine: Nearly 100 years on: A preliminary study of ayahuasca and psi.*" Abstracts of papers for the 35th International Conference of the Society for Psychical Research, Edinburgh. 2011.

65. Luna, Luis Eduardo, Pablo Amaringo. "*Ayahuasca Visions: The Religious Iconography of a Peruvian Shaman.*" Berkeley, CA: North Atlantic, 1991.

66. McKenna, Terence. Tryptamine Hallucinogens and Consciousness. Rec. Dec. 1982. Dolphin Tapes, n.d. Cassette.

67. Huxley, Aldous, Michael Horowitz, and Cynthia Palmer. *"Moksha: Aldous Huxley's Classic Writings on Psychedelics and the Visionary Experience"*. Rochester, VT: Park Street, 1999.

68. McKenna, Terence, perf. *"Psychedelic Salon Podcast #197: McNature"*. N.d. Matrix Masters. Web. 24 Dec. 2014.

69. Merkur, Daniel. *"The Psychedelic Sacrament: Manna, Meditation, and Mystical Experience"*. Rochester, VT: Park Street, 2001.

70. The Joe Rogan Experience.*"Podcast #356. Dan Hardy"*. YouTube.com. Retrieved 2014-11-13.

71. Benjamin, DR.*"Mushroom poisoning in infants and children: the Amanita pantherina/muscaria group"*. 1992. *Journal of Toxicology: Clinical Toxicology* 30 1: 13-22.

*Notes #47 and 51-54 were purposely excluded

About the Author

Brian Jackson is a rare breed of philosophical polymath. A true renaissance man, he enjoys writing and debating about alternative energy, religion, politics, sports, philosophy, and ancient history. He's previously contributed to content that's been featured by Current TV, Bloomberg Businessweek, and Daily Kos. Mr. Jackson also works as an income tax preparer, designs websites, and enjoys cycling in his spare time. He has a Bachelor's Degree in Finance and resides in central Florida with his cat, Buddy.

Contact Information
Website: PsychedelicAwakening.com
Email: brian@psychedelicawakening.com

www.ingramcontent.com/pod-product-compliance
Ingram Content Group UK Ltd.
Pitfield, Milton Keynes, MK11 3LW, UK
UKHW020141250726
13967UKWH00002B/789

9 781619 334243